D1190130

Required Reading Range
Module Reader

ART INSTITUTE LIBRARY

An AVA Book

Published by AVA Publishing
50 Bedford Square
London
WC1B 3DP
Tel: +44 0207 631 5600
Email: enquiries@avabooks.com

Distributed by Macmillan
Distribution
(ex-North America & Canada)
Brunel Road
Houndmills
Basingstoke
Hants
RG21 6XS
Tel (Home):
+44 (0) 1256 302 692
Fax (Home):
+44 (0) 1256 812 521
Tel (Export):
+44 (0) 1256 329 242
Fax (Export):
+44 (0) 1256 842 084

Distributed in the USA & Canada
by Macmillan
Orders:
MPS
P.O. Box 470
Gordonsville, VA 22942-8501
Phone: 888-330-8477
Fax: 800-672-2054
Email: orders@mpsvirginia.com

Returns:
MPS Returns Center
14301 Litchfield Drive
Orange, VA 22960
Phone: 888-330-8477

© Bloomsbury Publishing Plc
2013

All rights reserved. No part of this
publication may be reproduced,
stored in a retrieval system or
transmitted in any form or by any
means, electronic, mechanical,
photocopying, recording or
otherwise, without permission of
the copyright holder.

ISBN 978-2-940411-90-0
Printed in China

Library of Congress Cataloging-
in-Publication Data
Parish, Pat.
Pattern Cutting: The Architecture
of Fashion / Pat Parish p. cm.
Includes bibliographical
references and index.
ISBN: 9782940411900
(pbk. :alk. paper)
eISBN: 9782940447435
1. Dressmaking -- Pattern design.
2. Dressmaking -- Pattern design
-- Study and teaching. 3. Fashion
design -- Study and teaching.
TT520 .P377 2013

10 9 8 7 6 5 4 3 2 1

Design by Studio EMMI

Production by BMAG Production
Mgt. LLP, Singapore
Email: alicegoh@bmag.com.sg

All reasonable attempts have
been made to trace, clear and
credit the copyright holders of
the images reproduced in this
book. However, if any credits
have been inadvertently omitted,
the publisher will endeavour to
incorporate amendments in future
editions.

Opposite
<u>Yuichi Ozaki</u>
**Creative pattern cutting
can be immensely
rewarding, as this final
student collection shows.**

6   How to get the most out of this book

8   Introduction

10 Context
12   What is a pattern?
14   The role of the pattern cutter
16   Body shape and size
18   Measuring and mapping the body
26   Getting started

30 Pattern Fundamentals
32   From 3D to 2D – basic blocks
34   Darts in design
44   Panel lines for fit and flare control
50   Complex style lines
52   Adding flare
56   Adding volume

108 Sleeves, Collars and Circles
110 Sleeve fundamentals
112 Set-in sleeves
118 Grown-on sleeves
126 Sleeve cuffs
128 Collar fundamentals
130 One-piece collars
134 Two-piece collars
136 Circles and ruffles

138 Trousers
140 Trouser fundamentals
142 Standard fit
144 Adding pleats
148 Above-waist fitting
152 Below-waist fitting
156 Pockets, zips and finishes

60 Shape
62 Shape in design
64 Linear
68 Inverted triangle
72 Square
78 Trapeze
82 Hourglass
88 Dome
94 Lantern
98 Cocoon
102 Balloon

160 Sustainability and Fashion
162 Deconstructing hierarchies and traditions
164 Pattern cutting and waste
166 New horizons

172 **Appendix**
Conversion table
Glossary
Bibliography
Further recommended reading
Sustainable fabric suppliers
178 **Index**
180 **Acknowledgements and image credits**
181 **Working with ethics**

This book explores fashion design through creative pattern drafting, identifying key shapes and structures and translating them into 3D through a number of cutting, draping and construction processes.

Step-by-step instructions support annotated pattern diagrams. **Drawings and toile photographs** show the intended final outcome.

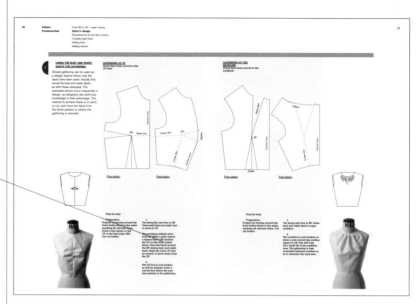

Troubleshooting sections offer handy tips on common areas of confusion or difficulty.

Additional notes are 'pinned' to the margins.

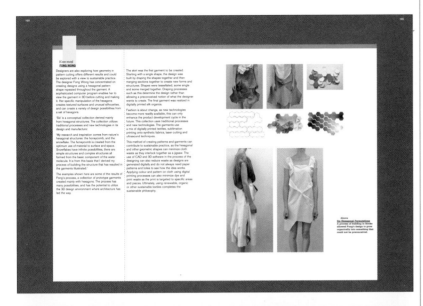

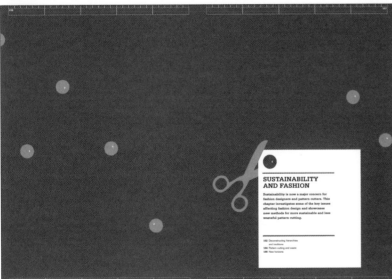

Case studies demonstrate how basic pattern cutting scenarios can be developed and manipulated in order to produce exciting new outcomes!

Chapter 6, '**Sustainability and Fashion**', addresses some important areas for consideration.

Abbreviations commonly used in this book

BP Bust Point

CB Centre Back

CBL Centre Back Line

CF Centre Front

CFL Centre Front Line

H Hip

LHS Left Hand Side

NP Neck Point (the point where the shoulder line meets the neckline)

RHS Right Hand Side

RSU Right Side Up (placing of a pattern when laying on cloth)

SL Sleeve Length

SP Shoulder Point (the point where the shoulder meets the sleeve crown)

SS Side Seam

UP Underarm Point

WSU Wrong Side Up (placing of pattern when laying on cloth)

XB Cross Back (measurement across upper back)

XF Cross Front (measurement across upper front)

INTRODUCTION

Fashion is situated within the creative industries and attracts many practitioners worldwide. As a discipline, fashion design can be highly inventive as it creates or reworks both subtle and extreme ways to clothe the body. Design and pattern cutting are often considered separate disciplines but they are inextricably linked. The designed garment can usually only be achieved through representation, and this is usually in the form of a pattern. Pattern cutting can even achieve high art status. Designers such as Madeleine Vionnet, Balenciaga, Alexander McQueen and Rei Kawakubo are just a few to have created fashion through inventive and expert pattern cutting.

Designers need to learn many skills in order to source, develop and refine design concepts. Equally, they need skills in order to test and present their ideas as prototypes, from which to measure some form of success or failure of the concept. The skill of pattern cutting is the vital link from concept to garment – it is the architecture of fashion.

This book approaches pattern cutting from a designer's perspective, encouraging an understanding of aesthetics which informs all areas of practice. Primarily intended for students of fashion design or individuals who are interested in creating their own clothes, it will be equally useful to fashion textile students who need to discover how their fabrics work.

The book includes basic fundamentals for beginners and includes some selected advanced pattern scenarios to inspire confidence to explore more complex designs. Frustration often arises when understanding and skills are insufficient for translating the concept into a physical item, and this book hopes to address this with clear, simple instructions and inspiring visuals.

Pattern cutting is a practical subject and as such the book will communicate techniques and processes through visual imagery. Simplicity is key in order to communicate seemingly complex processes, to 'demystify' this artful skill.

The ability to translate a design into pattern requires creative sensitivity to shape, proportion and balance of detail in relation to the whole, and this book supports development of these skills. The book explores pattern cutting in relation to design in a holistic way, identifying key areas such as shape and detail as a springboard to resolving design through pattern cutting. Methods to achieve fundamental shapes are offered in sequential diagrams, and details such as shoulders and collars are examined as part of the whole design concept. The holistic approach includes consideration of details such as cuffs, waistbands and garment finishes and how they contribute to the overall features of the designed garment. The shape and scale of these types of details can be a deciding factor in the success of a design.

The book also includes a history of pattern making and aims to underpin this practical subject with a theoretical context by examining the rise of consumerism and mass production and how this has influenced fashion garments.

The important issue of sustainable fashion needs consideration by designers, producers and consumers, and ways to integrate this in the process of design and pattern cutting are explored in the book. For example, clothes that fit well generally get used more and therefore have a longer life, which in turn delays its journey to landfill.

Consumers are more conscious of trends and style and can easily access seasonal collections on websites, and an informed consumer increasingly demands innovative design and well-fitted garments. This can be seen as an opportunity for design and pattern to be developed in tandem, exploring ways to minimize waste. Perhaps waste resulting from pattern shapes could be seen as a feature and incorporated into design, or reworking usual pattern cutting methods to reduce waste. It is hoped individuals will be inspired to find their own solutions.

Pattern cutting is often considered difficult and too methodical to be interesting. This book aims to show that it is neither of these things, rather that it can be creative, spontaneous and individual. We hope that the examples given here will inspire, encourage and give confidence to anyone wanting to move forward with their pattern cutting.

Above
Jane Bowler, Tufted
Grey Raincoat
Issues of sustainability are discussed in chapter 6. This coat by Jane Bowler (featured on pages 166–167) is made from recycled plastic.

1

Context

This chapter explains what pattern cutting is, and gives an overview of the evolution and history of pattern cutting and how measuring the body to create standard sizes developed pattern cutting systems. It reflects on changing body shape and size over decades and changing values of body aesthetics. Instructions on creating individual sets of body measurements are clearly explained and the tools needed to construct patterns are detailed. The role of the pattern cutter is also highlighted within the design and manufacturing processes.

12   What is a pattern?

14   The role of the pattern cutter

16   Body shape and size

18   Measuring and mapping the body

26   Getting started

What is a pattern?
The role of the pattern cutter
Body shape and size
Measuring and mapping the body
Getting started

WHAT IS A PATTERN?

A pattern can be described as a two-dimensional representation of a three-dimensional object. In clothing this would usually take the form of a front and back set of pattern shapes that, when cut in cloth and made up, form the garment. There are many ways to create a pattern, but the conventional way would be to use a set of blocks of a specific size to represent fundamental shapes and sections of the body, (such as the bodice, sleeve, skirt and trouser) and use these as the basic pattern piece outlines. There are a variety of methods to create blocks and this is covered by several authors of pattern books. I have for this book used the blocks created from Winifred Aldrich's system, 'Metric Pattern Cutting for Women's Wear', as I have found it most compatible with the tailor's dummy.

EXPLORING GARMENTS THROUGH DECONSTRUCTION

It can be useful for beginners to deconstruct old garments in order to understand how they look when complete and how they look when in pattern pieces. Using old clothes, follow these steps:

- Photograph or draw front, back and sides of the garment, including details such as waistbands, collars, cuffs and pockets.
- Photograph the inside, noting how it is constructed and finished.
- Chalk or tack centre back, centre front, bust line, waist and hip lines. Mark the centres of collars at centre back, and sleeve centre lines by folding in half.
- Carefully unpick one half of the garment (or the whole if you prefer). Photograph or draw each separate pattern piece as you go.
- Press carefully so as not to stretch the fragile pieces at the edges and trace around the shapes.

You may then understand how the pattern shapes combine to create the garment.

BLOCKS

Blocks are created in card or plastic and are used as templates for tracing around. It is best to prepare the block shape with adjustments for the intended basic shape and general fit included. Blocks are usually generous in width so fitted garments will need to be adjusted accordingly. There are no specific rules of how much to adjust, this is entirely down to the intended design outcome.

The paper pattern of the general shape is then pinned onto the tailor's dummy, where design lines can be drawn onto it using a soft pencil, black tape or specialist removable tape. This sequence is applied in most instances.

Patterns and blocks can also be developed in 3D using draping on a tailor's dummy. This method is covered in more detail later in the book.

Seasonal designs usually require new shapes but it is common practice to use well established blocks and patterns from season to season; tried and tested patterns can save a lot of time! Designers have a 'signature' style or design 'handwriting' which can be recognizable, but the need for new ideas can mean having to find new concepts and new shapes – specially created block shapes can form the foundation to a collection and hold a design concept together.

The amount of time spent developing patterns depends on the industry level. In haute couture, for example, it is reasonable to spend hours on this stage, whereas for designers in larger companies, time and money is of the essence and there is less opportunity for toiling and fitting.

COMPUTERS AND PATTERN CUTTING

When computer software is used in pattern cutting, it is usually called CAD/CAM (Computer Aided Design and Computer Aided Manufacture). The majority of medium and large fashion companies will use CAD/CAM as it is much quicker. It is also easy to maintain accuracy with CAD/CAM as it can measure and work to fine decimal points. Similarly, storage of patterns is easy and, depending on the size of the hard drive, computers can hold many thousands of patterns in perfect condition.

Other benefits include being able to reproduce multiple copies quickly and accurately, and reduced waste.

The main prerequisites for digitized patterns are a computer, software, a digitizer for programmes (such as Gerber Accumark) so that paper patterns can be digitized and uploaded onto the computer, and a plotter printer if the pattern is to be printed off. Patterns can be scanned and then digitized but will need to be checked carefully for accuracy, and this is not the usual method employed by industry.

Students are introduced to CAD/CAM on most fashion design courses and are shown the benefits of creating patterns digitally. In some instances, a computer may not be the best method of creating a pattern, so it is essential to have experience of both digital and hand-drawn methods. This book concentrates on mainly flat pattern cutting using traditional methods which can be practised using traditional tools; however, examples of work created using computer software are included in Chapter 6.

Left
<u>Margherita Mazzola</u>
Pattern cutting and
transforming an idea from 2D
into 3D is an essential skill for
any aspiring fashion designer.

What is a pattern?
The role of the pattern cutter
Body shape and size
Measuring and mapping the body
Getting started

THE ROLE OF THE PATTERN CUTTER

1

The pattern cutter enables the design to be made, and is crucial to the design and make process. Their skills provide the template (pattern) from which production can occur. There are many designers who work from the pattern to create a design, or at least need to work in 3D with cloth to see design potential. Alexander McQueen, for example, worked in 3D: 'I design from the side, that way I get the worst angle of the body. You've got all the worst lumps and bumps, the S-bend of the back, the bum. That way I get a cut and proportion and silhouette that works all the way around the body'.

Ruth Faulkener

A lot of designers think in 3D – obviously you can only draw something that's flat, so the job of a pattern cutter is to take that sketch and bring it to life in a series of pattern pieces... There is a creative dialogue which goes on which gives a better product... it is all about the shape.

WORKING IN 3D

A design needs to be interpreted from a sketch and this is easier if you are the designer cutting your own pattern – you have the vision of what you want. However, if you are cutting a pattern from another designer's sketch you need to be able to 'feel' the design, to get a sense of shape, scale, proportion and balance. Interpreting the design in this way is a crucial part of the development of the garment. A dialogue with the designer (if not yourself) is useful as this can help to understand the design concept.

The pattern cutter is also responsible for making corrections after fittings and cutting the production pattern, which will include interlinings, button slopers and any relevant parts of the garment. Skills in CAD and specific pattern cutting software are integral to pattern cutting learning and application.

Pattern cutting is an honourable and desirable career, and despite at this time many clothes being cut and produced in other countries, the benefits of 'in-house' pattern cutters are countless. It is evident in the design room hierarchy that the pattern cutter is highly valued.

AN INTERVIEW WITH A PATTERN CUTTER: JACQUIE BOUNSALL

What training did you have?

I did a BA (Hons) in Fashion Design and Textiles at Saint Martins in London. I also did an intensive six-month course at London College of Fashion in Pattern Cutting for people who worked in the industry.

In your opinion, what skills or attributes do you think a pattern cutter needs?

You need patience and a good eye for interpreting 2D images. You also need to be able to work as part of a team.

Where did you learn most of your skills?

My mother used to make clothes for my sister and I and we started making our own clothes from dress patterns when we were young. The course at LCF showed me how to use industrial techniques, but I really learnt how to pattern cut in my first job where I had a very knowledgeable boss. The machinists were always very helpful with tips and better ways of constructing something.

What do you think is the most difficult part of pattern cutting?

Most people can draw a sketch of a garment, but it requires knowledge of the human form to translate that into a wearable garment. There are endless ground rules that can be broken. I think it is essential to understand the basics, such as straight grain and dart manipulation, so that you know when you can move away from them.

What process or steps do you take to interpret a design successfully?

It is essential to talk through a sketch with the designer because you can easily misinterpret something. Designers have often done weeks of research to get to a final design so it saves time if they show you their storyboards. It is important to understand the chosen fabric – this can change the volume of your pattern as different fabrics behave differently. I would always create a first toile as quickly as possible, usually in fabric left from a previous collection that is nearest to the one in the design. It would ideally be shown on a model or stand of the correct size. I would then discuss the shape with the designer to make sure they are happy with it. At this stage they should tell you if you have interpreted the design accurately, and if not, give you a list of amendments.

What do you think makes a great pattern cutter?

I have talked about patience and a visual eye, but you have to be open to change as a pattern cutter. There are always new ways of approaching something. You never stop learning.

Do you think a pattern should influence a design?

A pattern can influence a design for the better when there has been a miscommunication, or perhaps at the toile stage when the pattern cutter or designer can see a better way of doing something, but the design ideas are often part of a collection and they need to string together.

In industry do you work alone or as a team?

Pattern cutters are part of a team. The structure of each business can be different, but the basic set-up is usually the designer provides the concept, the pattern cutter turns that into a 3D garment with the aid of a machinist.

What pattern cutting tips or advice would you give to readers?

Always mark your patterns with clear cutting instructions and notches. Do not try to save time by imagining what something will look like, take the time to make it up. It always saves time in the end and this is also the stage where you can try out techniques.

16   Context

What is a pattern?
The role of the pattern cutter
Body shape and size
Measuring and mapping the body
Getting started

BODY SHAPE AND SIZE

Body shapes and sizes have changed over the centuries largely due to changes in people's health and nutrition, adoption of western lifestyles and mixing of ethnic races. Historically, tailors noted that there were several noticeable body types to differentiate from, and adjusted fitting accordingly. By the nineteenth century, images of the body were being documented with photography in Europe and further afield, and this led to a better understanding of body form. The art of tailoring became a science, and new methods for mapping the body were developed.

ANTHROPOMETRY

From the Greek, *anthro* meaning 'man' and *metron* meaning 'measure', this is a discipline developed in the nineteenth century, with an interest in systematic descriptions of populations. Basic anthropometric measurements include ratios such as upper arm to lower arm, and breadth to length.

CHANGING SHAPES

The female ideal has witnessed many different shapes and sizes since the turn of the century and these changes are commonly linked to cultural changes, particularly in the West where fashion has been dominant. The timeline below offers an overview of some of the 'ideal' shapes and sizes.

MEASURING SYSTEMS

Measuring became complicated with increasing body measurements, and several systems were adopted, some even patented, such as McDowell's adjustable pattern-plates for drafting garments. Around the mid-nineteenth century, measurements became more refined and were documented into symmetrical divisions of the body, identifying specifics such as top sleeve and under sleeve.

The main systems were divisional (dividing major measurements proportionally), direct measurements (noting most points on the body and combination) or a combination of both systems. Systems varied between mathematical and anthropometric systems.

1890–1910
Edwardian beauties were buxom and small waisted, with the typical hourglass figure.

1920s
The jazz age of music brought freedom from the corset and clothes allowed the body to move. Sleek boyish shapes were fashionable.

1930s
Utopian living, exercise and cleaner living brought healthy, lean bodies.

1940s
Betty Grable, a popular pin-up during the Second World War, had a body of balanced proportions. This perhaps reflected the traditional values and conservatism in society during the war years?

3D BODY SCANNERS

Computers offer an opportunity to measure the body in 3D without the need for tape measures. The body is scanned for critical measurements so that individual bodies can be catered for and measurements applied to bespoke patterns.

SIZING

The ability to produce patterns in different sizes was helped by the invention of graduated scales by Guillaume Compaing around 1828, and the combination of this system and new body measuring techniques meant patterns could be scaled up or down. This grading is now done by computer although there are still highly skilled paper graders working to similar systems of incremental sizing and tolerances.

Anne Klein
Clothes aren't going to change the world. The women who wear them will.

1950s
Marilyn Monroe epitomized the full curved female figure, reflecting domesticity and glamour.

1960s
Androgynous body shapes such as Twiggy's and Mia Farrow's (pictured here) became popular in a time of civil rights and a new wave of feminism.

1970s
A fuller figure such as Farah Fawcett's (shown here with her fellow Charlie's Angels) became popular during this period of sexual revolution.

1980s
A physical fitness explosion brought power and sexuality to the female form. Brigitte Nielsen (shown here) was just one of many actresses at this time who were happy to put their bodies on show.

1990s and beyond
Kate Moss and her fellow 'supermodels' embody the idea of globalization. There is still an ongoing debate about model size.

What is a pattern?
The role of the pattern cutter
Body shape and size
Measuring and mapping the body
Getting started

MEASURING AND MAPPING THE BODY

There are many systems for creating the blocks from which patterns are made. All require fundamental body measurements and are gathered in a similar way. In industry, blocks are created to standard sizes and are usually for a UK size 12 (US size 8), but different countries have other standard sizing, although they are still likely to use similar measuring systems.

A design will invariably have its own particular measurements in relation to the body so no standard can be applied to individual designs.

Measuring around the body with a tape measure, referencing measurements against an existing garment before cutting a pattern from a block helps to determine the scale, proportion and balance of the design.

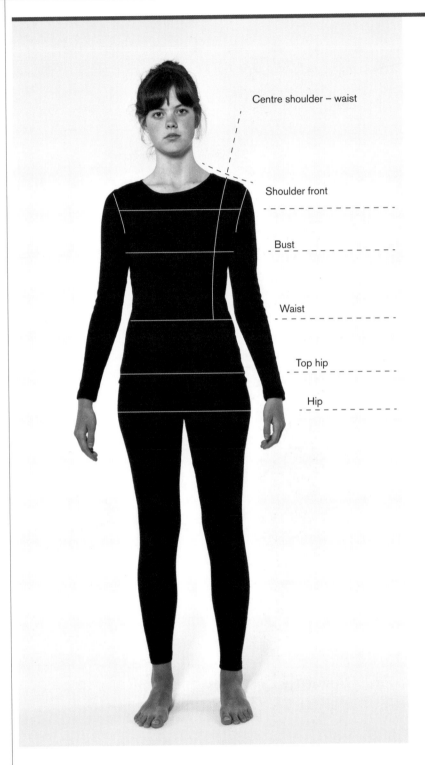

Centre shoulder – waist

Shoulder front

Bust

Waist

Top hip

Hip

Front body measurements

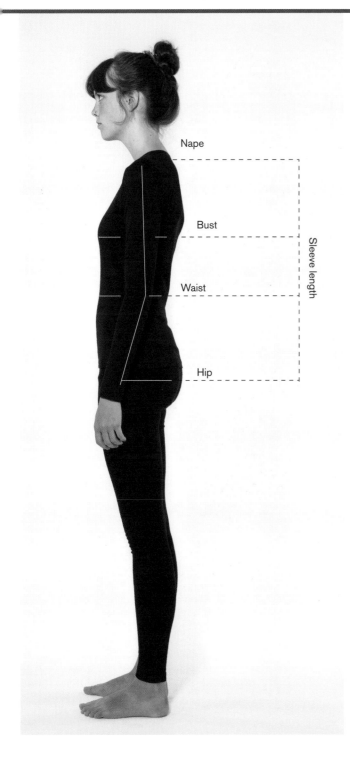

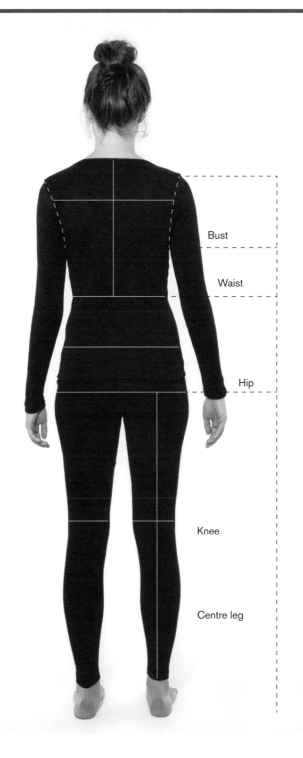

Side body measurements

Back body measurements

What is a pattern?
The role of the pattern cutter
Body shape and size
Measuring and mapping the body
Getting started

NATURAL WAISTLINE

When measuring the body, it can be helpful to have tape or ribbon tied at the natural waistline.

1

MEASURING FOR A BODICE BLOCK

The following are measured:

- Centre back line (CB) measured from the nape of the neck (bottom where it bends) to the waist (where the tape is).

- Waist measurement, not tight.

- Bust – keep the tape measure level and over the Bust Point (BP).

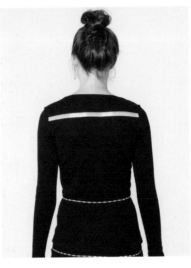

- Cross back – 10cm down the CB line measure across the width of the back to where the arm begins.

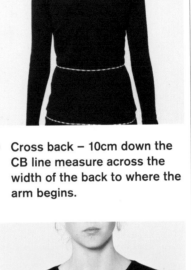

- Cross front – about halfway between shoulder and bust line measure across to where the arm dips in slightly, so that when you move the arm forward it is not restricted.

- Shoulder point (SP) to (SP).

- Front Centre Shoulder (CS) over bust to waist.
- Back Centre Shoulder (CS) over shoulder blade to waist.

Extra measurements can be taken such as above and below the bust line for fitted strapless bodices.

MEASURING FOR A SLEEVE BLOCK

The following are measured:

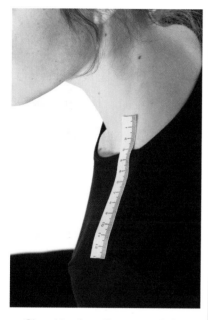

- **Shoulder length** – a straight line from the base of the neck to where the arm bends down.

- **Nape–Elbow–Wrist** – CB nape diagonally across the back to elbow and wrist, keeping the arm gently bent.

- **Shoulder–Elbow–Wrist** – measure from the top centre of the sleeve where it meets the shoulder line, diagonally across the elbow and to the wrist with the arm gently bent.

- **Top arm** – measure a curved line rising upwards slightly around the full part of the top arm.

- **Elbow** – measure around the elbow with the arm slightly bent.

- **Wrist (at wrist bone level)** – do not make too tight as the sleeve moves up the arm when it is raised.

Extra measurements above and below the elbow are useful for fitted sleeves.

What is a pattern?
The role of the pattern cutter
Body shape and size
Measuring and mapping the body
Getting started

1

MEASURING FOR A SKIRT BLOCK

The following are measured:

- **Waist (as for bodice).**

- **Top hip – a level measurement between the hip and waist, about 15cm down the side of the body.**

- **Hip – a level measurement around the hip, about 21–22cm down the side of the body from the waist.**

- **Waist to knee – measure down the side of the body from the waist.**

For individual blocks and patterns, if the thigh area is greater than the hip then use this measurement.

MEASURING FOR A TROUSER BLOCK

The following are measured:

- **Waist (as bodice).**
- **Hip (as skirt).**
- **Top hip (as skirt).**

- **Outside leg.**
- **Inside leg.**

- **Body rise – IMPORTANT measurement – the length of the body from waist to level surface when seated.**

  Note: Use a ruler, set square or rigid rule and measure at the side.

For high-waist trousers or skirts, measure above waist. For low-waist trousers, measure at the level wanted.

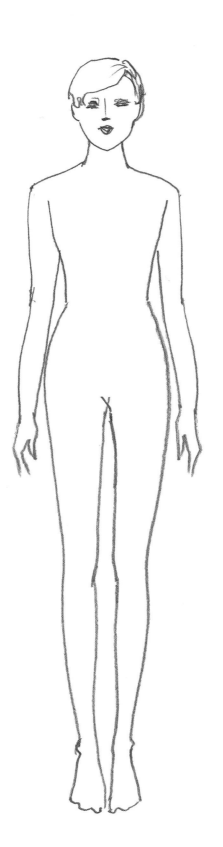

Use photocopies of this
outline to help with your
own measuring.

What is a pattern?
The role of the pattern cutter
Body shape and size
Measuring and mapping the body
Getting started

SIZE CHARTS

1

Manufacturers supply designers with their own size charts but the examples given here are a good indication of how the body measurements translate to the block.

A conversion table from cm to inches is shown on page 172.

WOMEN'S SIZE CHART (METRIC) UK SIZE

	8	10
Height	157.2	159.6
Bust	80	84
Under bust	61	66
Waist	60	64
Hip	87	90.5
Top hip	79.5	84
Shoulder	11.5	11.7
Neck	34	35
Nape to waist at CB	38.8	40.4
X back	31.8	32
X front (chest)	28	29.8
Sleeve length (top)	56.2	57.1
Underarm length	42.8	43.1
Armhole (scye)	38.6	40.6
Top arm (bicep)	22.9	24.7
Wrist	15	15.2
Elbow	21.9	23.7
Waist to knee (CB)	61	61
Waist to ankle (CB)	94	94
CB nape to floor	136	138
Outside leg	99	100.5
Inside leg	74	74
Body rise	26.8	27.9

UK SIZING EQUIVALENTS FOR OTHER COUNTRIES

UK	6	8
USA	2	4
Spain/France	34	36
Italy	38	40
Germany	32	34
Japan	3	5

12	14	16
162	164.4	166.8
88	93	96
71	76	81
68	73	76
95	99.5	102
89	94	96
11.9	12.1	12.3
36	37	38
41	41.6	42.2
33	34.2	35.6
31	32.2	33.4
58	58.9	59.8
43.5	43.9	44.3
42.6	44.6	46.6
26.5	28.3	30.1
16	16.6	17.6
25.5	27.3	29.1
61.5	61.5	61.5
95	95	95
140	142	144
102	103.5	105
74.5	74.5	75
29	30.1	31.2

10	12	14	16	18	20	22
6	8	10	12	14	16	18
38	40	42	44	46	48	50
42	44	46	48	50	52	54
36	38	40	42	44	46	48
7	9	11	13	15	17	19

26   Context

What is a pattern?
The role of the pattern cutter
Body shape and size
Measuring and mapping the body
Getting started

GETTING STARTED

1

Pattern cutting requires specific tools. Those listed here are easily acquired. Experienced pattern cutters are able to draw curves freehand as they know exactly where they want the curve to be, but the tools are helpful and give good results. A pattern master is an essential tool as it has straight and curved lines, graduated parallel and curved lines with 5mm and 1cm increments for adding seam allowance quickly and efficiently, and 90 and 45 degree angles and lines for squaring lines and bias grain marking.

To start with, a basic set of tools is needed, and as you progress other tools can be added.

ESSENTIAL TOOLS

The following are measured:

1. Pattern master (metric)
2. Set of French curves
3. Soft-ended metric tape measure
4. Tracing wheel
5. Pattern drill
6. Pattern notcher
7. Awl
8. Paper and card scissors
9. Fabric scissors
10. Pins
11. Tailor's chalk
12. Short straight metal ruler
13. Snippers

OTHER USEFUL TOOLS

- Long straight metal metre ruler
- Grading ruler
- Hip curves, collar curves
- Set squares
- Pattern hole punch
- Pattern hooks (available large and small)
- Large cutting mat
- Masking tape, magic tape and Pritt Stick
- Unpicker
- Scalpel
- Pattern paper and card
- Set of H and HB pencils, sharpeners and erasers, and general coloured pens

Narciso Rodriguez
What I relate to is the creation of form from structure and material. Although I don't use direct architectural references in my work, I approach designing a garment in much the same way as an architect designs a building.

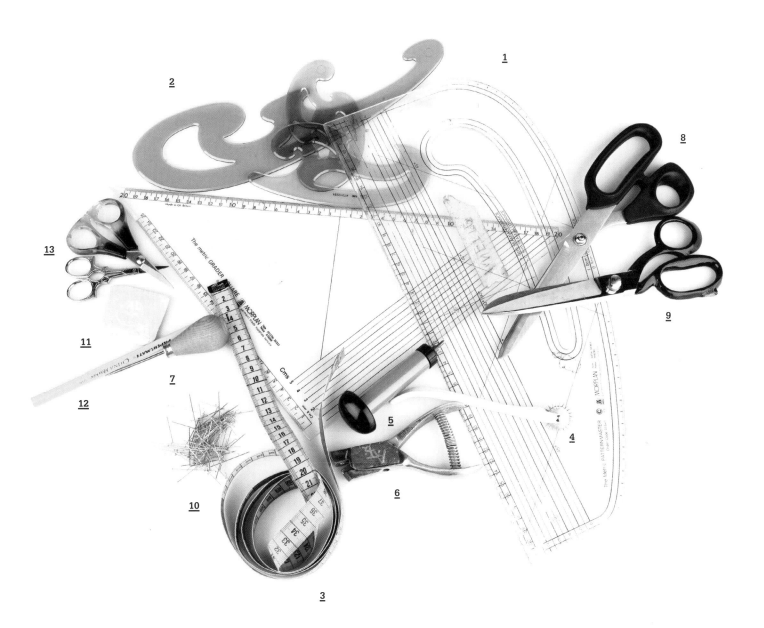

What is a pattern?
The role of the pattern cutter
Body shape and size
Measuring and mapping the body
Getting started

1

WHAT THE TOOLS DO

1.
Pattern master

This is a transparent all-in-one tool with a straight-edge ruler, short grading ruler, 90 and 45 degree markers for squaring lines and finding the bias grain, and various curves inside and outside helpful in drawing armholes, necklines, hip curves, hem curves and others. The parallel incremental lines of 5mm and 1cm can be used to add seam allowances on straight and curved lines.

2.
Set of French curves

If other specialist curves are not available, these curves are a good substitute as they offer a wide variety of small and longer curves which can be used for necklines, armholes, collars and cuffs, or general curved line drafting.

3.
Soft-ended tape measure

A soft-ended tape measure allows it to bend at the end, essential for measuring curved lines accurately (although one could use a measure from A–B anywhere on a tape measure). It is used for measuring any lengths from straight to curved lines on the body, tailor's dummy and pattern.

4.
Tracing wheel

A tool for transferring pattern information from one piece of paper or card to another. Tracing lines from a pattern with the tool leaves spiked indentations on the new sheet of paper below which are then retraced (copied). This tool is vital for making corrections at drafting and fitting.

5.
Pattern drill

This is also referred to as a 'mushroom'. Drill parts are available in 4 and 6mm sizes and drill small holes to mark positions on a pattern such as dart ends and sewing ends, corners that will often need to be cut, position of pockets, and button and buttonhole positions.

6.
Pattern notcher

Cuts out a small u or v shape from the paper to indicate seam allowance and balance marks. These notched positions are cut into the fabric and should not be deep, no more than 4mm.

7.
Awl

Can be used to mark information from a pattern drill (mushroom) position by drilling a small hole in fabric. It actually separates the yarns as the end is not needle-sharp. It can also be used when pivoting darts and patterns and marking long lines such as CF, CB and sleeve, for example.

8., 9.
Paper and card and fabric scissors

It is better to have long paper scissors to cut long smooth lines. Card scissors are usually shorter and have slightly serrated edges which grip the card. Fabric scissors must be kept separate from paper scissors as paper blunts them. Fabric scissors should have some weight and handles that are comfortable to use. They must also have length of at least 25cm. Heavy solid blades can be sharpened, but it can be more convenient to buy new when needed.

10.
Pins

Pins hold paper together, secure paper to fabric and secure patterns to the dummy.

11.
Tailor's chalk (or thin cotton tape/ specialist removable tape)

Use chalk with a sharp edge to trace around patterns onto cloth and mark positions of dart ends, pockets etc. Keep the edge sharp by shaving with a pair of scissors or blade regularly. A chalk dispenser can save time as it does not blunt.

The tape is used for marking style lines on a pattern or toile instead of using a pencil or pen. Pin the tape where you want it, stand back and see what you have drawn with the tape – it is moveable so can be adjusted. The specialist tape is striped black and white and is easily reused.

12.
Short metal ruler

Can help steady drawing of short straight lines and cutting short lines with a scalpel.

13.
Snippers

Small, 'snipper' scissors are useful for tidying up loose threads and small pieces of fabric.

Long metal metric ruler

Metal rulers are preferable to plastic or wooden ones as they do not warp. They are used in a variety of ways, for drawing long lines in dresses, coats and trousers (in fact, any line longer than the pattern master). They can also be used for measuring and smoothing fabric across a table, and for cutting long lines with a scalpel.

Grading ruler

A grading ruler has incremental measurements for moving lines and spaces up or down in scale, which helps to change the size of a pattern. It is usually only used when the pattern is complete, although it can be used as a substitute pattern master for seam allowances.

Hip curves and collar curves

Long curved rulers that can be helpful when drawing hips, long collars and hemline curves. Particularly useful in tailoring.

Set squares

Similar function to a pattern master but more limiting without curves. Useful for drawing angles.

Pattern hole punch and pattern hooks

Makes medium holes for pattern hooks. Pattern hooks thread through the pattern to keep all parts together and to hang up.

Cutting mat

If using a scalpel, this will protect surfaces from being damaged and will not blunt the blade.

Masking tape, magic tape and Pritt Stick

Masking tape is used to hold paper patterns together for checking on the tailor's dummy. It is easily removed and can also be a substitute for small areas of calico when making alterations during fittings. Magic tape is invisible, durable and can be drawn and written on. Pritt Stick is a useful aid to joining paper together and can be repositioned before the glue sets.

Unpicker and scalpel

The unpicker has a covered point on one side to help slide between fabric to unpick stitches and not tear the fabric; however, it is a dangerous tool as it can easily slip. A scalpel can do the same sort of job, but care is important. It is also used for cutting lines with a ruler on a mat. Note: If the stitches are not too close try unpicking by pulling and snapping the threads and unravelling – this is a method sample machinists often use.

Pattern paper and card

Pattern paper and card comes in different weights, so choose the weight most workable. Too thin pattern paper tears and too thick does not fold and bend easily. I prefer plain paper to spot and cross as I think the crosses interfere with the visual quality of the pattern, and can be misleading, but this is all down to preference and availability.

Pencils and other stationery

The best pencils are fine and sharp, such as H. Drawing trial style lines on a pattern, especially if it is on the dummy, is best done with a softer pencil, such as HB or B. You do not have to press hard to get a mark. Once satisfied, the line can be retraced using a fine pencil. Marker pens instantly show areas of importance. Soft putty rubbers are best as they are less likely to tear the fabric when erasing.

Pattern Fundamentals

This chapter demonstrates how pattern blocks translate 3D to 2D. One of the most important fundamentals – identifying where the bust dart position can be and how to move it around the body – is explained, and basic fundamentals of how to introduce flare and volume are demonstrated in a skirt and sleeve. Once these principles are understood, more complex and creative pattern cutting can be achieved.

32 From 3D to 2D – basic blocks

34 Darts in design

44 Panel lines for fit and flare control

50 Complex style lines

52 Adding flare

56 Adding volume

32 **Pattern Fundamentals**

From 3D to 2D – basic blocks
Darts in design
Panel lines for fit and flare control
Complex style lines
Adding flare
Adding volume

FROM 3D TO 2D – BASIC BLOCKS

2

Measurements from the body are used to create flat 2D templates called blocks. These represent the body shape in its simplest form. These blocks are referred to as basic blocks because more developed shapes created by designers and manufacturers can be created over time and successful shapes can become blocks from which seasonal collections can be developed.

BLOCKS

Blocks are usually made from card or plastic and can be traced around quickly when preparing for pattern development.

DARTS

The blocks have darts to create shape over the bust, shoulder and hips, and to reduce the waist.

A dartless block has the darts spread around the bodice and cannot be tight fitting unless the fabric has stretch. Cutting the shape on the bias of the fabric can help to 'stretch' over the bust.

FITTING

The blocks have tolerance, meaning they are bigger than standard size measurements to allow for movement and comfort.

When starting a pattern from a block, the fit should be established and the pattern should be adjusted accordingly, by taking it in or out at the side seam. If a very tight fit or fabrics with stretch yarn are used, then it will be necessary to also increase the waist dart.

EXAMPLES OF A SKIRT BLOCK

All of these diagrams were created using Winifred Aldrich's system. There are alternative block making systems.

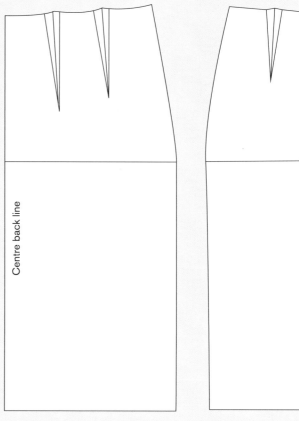

Basic back skirt block

Basic front skirt block

 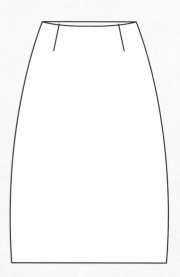

Flat drawing of made-up skirt

EXAMPLE OF BODICE BLOCK

EXAMPLE OF A SLEEVE BLOCK

HALF AND HALF
Blocks are cut to represent half the body as it is assumed the body is equal both sides. The sleeve is in full as there are differences between the back and front.

Shoulder dart

Bust dart

Centre back line

Waist dart

Waist

Centre front line

Waist dart

Waist

Crown

B | F

Centre line

Elbow

Wrist

Basic back bodice block

Basic front bodice block

Basic sleeve block

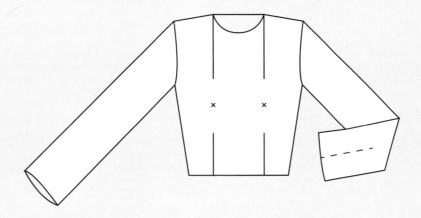

Flat drawing of made-up bodice and sleeve

34   **Pattern Fundamentals**   From 3D to 2D – basic blocks
Darts in design
Panel lines for fit and flare control
Complex style lines
Adding flare to a pattern
Adding volume

DARTS IN DESIGN

2

Bust darts need to be considered when developing a pattern for a design as they represent shaping over the bust. In many instances the bust dart is in the side seam as it is least obvious and slightly hidden by the arm. Once the fundamentals are understood then darts can be easily incorporated into the design and can even be a design feature. The deconstructionist movement, for example, turned construction of darts inside out, and bust and other darts were exposed and celebrated as an integral part of a design.

BUST DARTS

The five positions of the bust dart all take the dart to an outside edge and do not change the general characteristics of the block. Whatever you change in a pattern, the CF, CB and waist position are constants and can never change from their original position. If the dart is moved to the CF line it will break the CF line and will need to be seamed.

Five basic dart positions that do not alter the CF line are: centre shoulder, neck, side seam, hem and armhole.

MOVING THE BUST DART

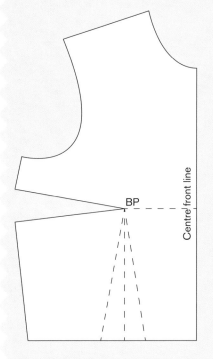

Prep pattern showing slash line
from BP to CF (see also p36)

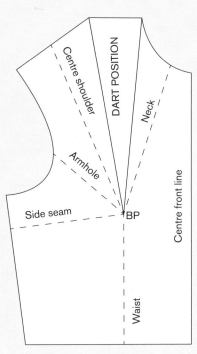

Prep pattern showing the five
dart positions opposite

Step-by-step:

1.
Trace around the front bodice block to the waist or length of the garment. Mark and draw onto the tracing all relevant information from the block, making sure the waistline is marked.

2.
Mark the new position of the dart drawing a line to meet bust point (BP).

3.
Cut along the new line from the outside edge to the bust point (BP), fold existing dart away so it appears in the new position, or pivot existing dart closed to new position. The pivoting of darts is best used when more confident with understanding the technique, and having explored the 'cut and close' method first.

4.
Retrace the bodice with the new dart position making sure all information is transferred.

FIVE BASIC BUST DART POSITIONS

Shoulder

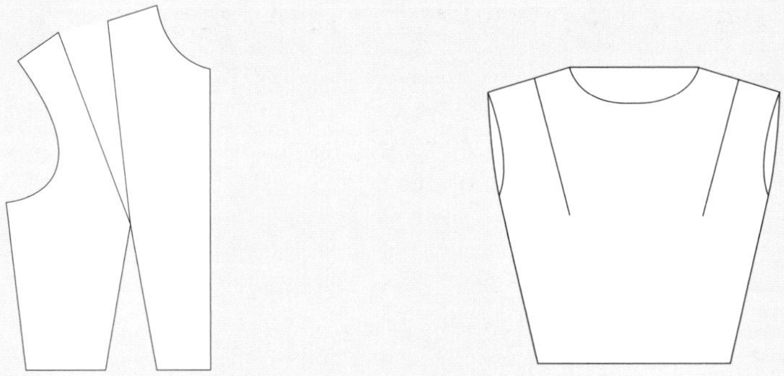

Neck

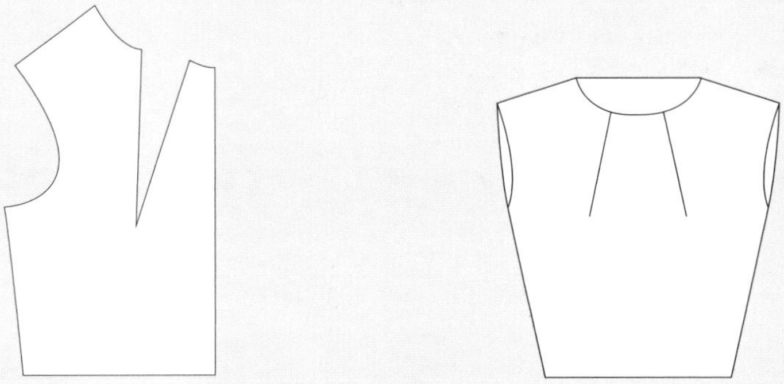

Side seam

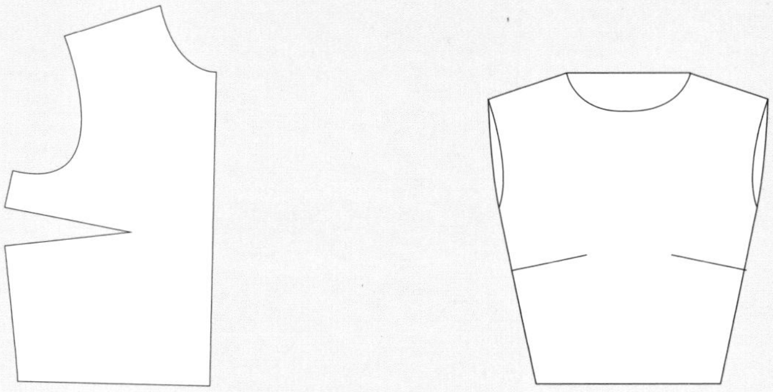

Hem or waist

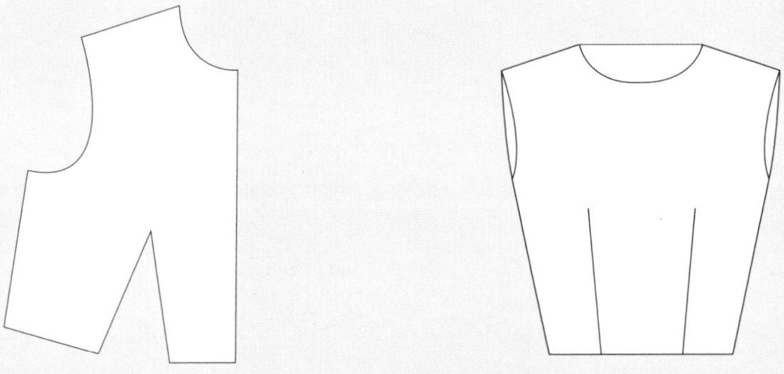

Armhole

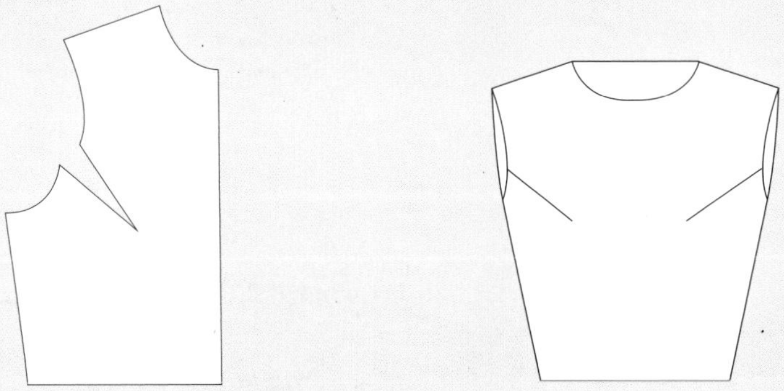

36   Pattern   From 3D to 2D – basic blocks
      Fundamentals   **Darts in design**
                       Panel lines for fit and flare control
                       Complex style lines
                       Adding flare
                       Adding volume

2

USING THE BUST AND WAIST DARTS FOR GATHERING

Simple gathering can be used as a design feature where only the darts have been used. Usually this would be bust and waist darts, as with these examples. The examples shown occur frequently in design, as designers use technical knowledge to best advantage. The method to achieve these is to pivot, or cut, and move the darts from the block position to where the gathering is intended.

GATHERING AT CF
(Darts have been moved to the CF line)

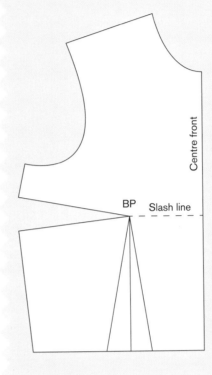

Prep pattern

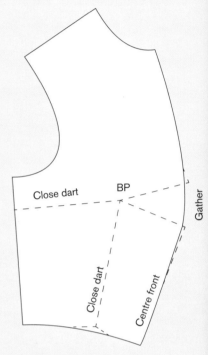

Final pattern

Step-by-step:

Preparation
Prepare by tracing around the front bodice block to the waist marking all relevant darts. Draw a line square to the CF to the bust point (BP). Cut out bodice.

1.
Cut along the new line to BP. Close both bust and waist dart to move to CF.

The pivoting method: pivot from BP. Mark a point where a square line to BP touches the CF on the front bodice block. Pivot the block around the BP closing bust and waist darts. Keep the lower CF line as normal, so pivot away from the CF.

2.
The CF line is now broken so will be seamed. Draw a curved line where the new dart position is for gathering.

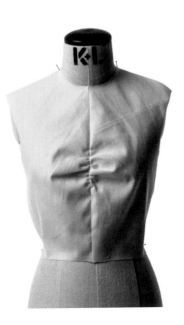

**GATHERING AT THE
NECKLINE**
(Darts have been moved to the
neckline)

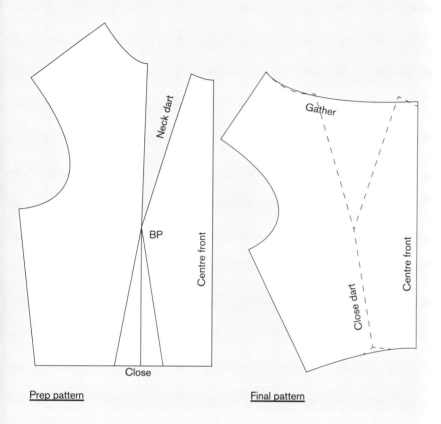

Prep pattern   Final pattern

Step-by-step:

Preparation
Prepare by tracing around the
front bodice block to the waist,
marking all relevant darts. Cut
out bodice.

1.
Cut along new line to BP. Close
bust and waist darts to open
neckline.

2.
The neckline is now broken so
draw a new curved line ending
square to CF, this will trim
off a small bit of the neckline
area. The gathering is best
controlled between notches so
as to maintain the neck size.

38   **Pattern Fundamentals**   From 3D to 2D – basic blocks
Darts in design
Panel lines for fit and flare control
Complex style lines
Adding flare
Adding volume

DARTS INCORPORATED INTO DESIGN

2

Darts can be used as a design feature in many ways. Here, we demonstrate three examples which may inspire experimentation.

DIAMOND INSET

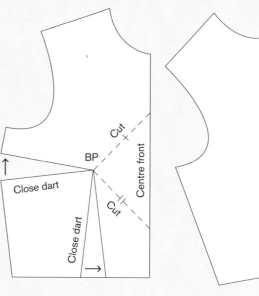

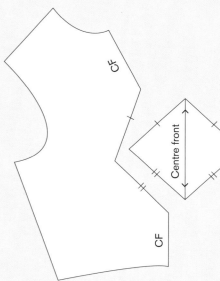

Prep pattern   Final pattern

Step-by-step

1.
Trace around the bodice block to the waist, with the bust dart in the side seam. The pattern can initially be developed as a half-pattern.

2.
Draw in two diagonal lines to the BP starting from the CF line to form half a diamond shape. Use a set square to the CF through the BP, marking a point on the CF line. The new lines can be measured equidistant above and below this point.

3.
Mark balance notches along these lines before cutting and separating from the body. Redraw this inset on the fold of paper to create a whole piece. Transfer all information onto the new pattern pieces.

4.
Close bust and waist darts away – this will transfer the shaping into the lines of the diamond shape.

CF DART AND INSET PANEL

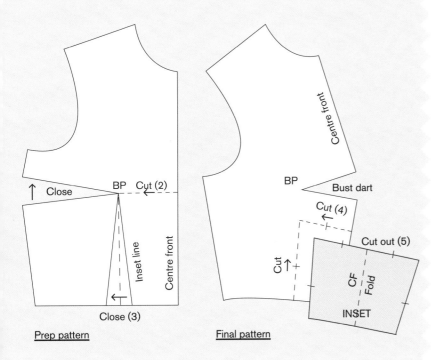

Prep pattern Final pattern

Step-by-step

1.
Prepare by tracing around bodice block to waist, with bust dart in side seam. Mark all relevant information.

2.
Square a line from CF to BP for the new bust dart position. Cut along this new line to BP.

3.
Close waist dart. Use the dart line as a guide for the inset panel.

4.
Square a line to the CF parallel and a few centimetres below the new dart position.

5.
Mark balance points on the panel to be separated. Cut out and place CF on fold of paper so that the inset is a whole piece. Transfer information.

6.
The finished pattern will have bust dart in the CF and the waist dart in the inset panel lines.

40   **Pattern**
       Fundamentals

From 3D to 2D – basic blocks
Darts in design
Panel lines for fit and flare control
Complex style lines
Adding flare
Adding volume

2

ASYMMETRICAL CURVED DART LINES

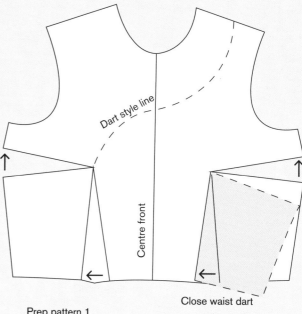

Dart style line

Centre front

Close waist dart

Prep pattern 1

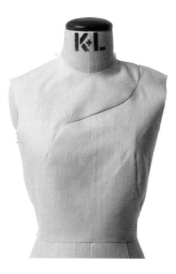

Step-by-step

1.
Trace around the bodice block to the waist, with bust dart in the side seam and CF on the fold of the paper, creating a whole front as the diagram shows. Mark all relevant information from the block with a tracing wheel so it appears on the underside of the paper. Open the paper and draw in all the information lines.

2.
Draw in the upper style line from the shoulder to the BP, in a good curve across the pattern so that it crosses the CF line. This can be done by placing the pattern on the tailor's dummy and marking the lines with tape and transferring later or simply drawing the lines on the flat pattern.

3.
Cut along this new line to BP. Close the waist dart to BP so that all waist shaping is transferred into the dart style line.

4.
Prepare the other side for the new style line bust and waist dart transfer by cutting open the side bust dart and closing the waist dart to BP. This will increase the side bust dart.

5.
Draw in the new curved style line from the lower side seam to BP, either on the tailor's dummy or flat.

6.
Complete the pattern by cutting along the new lower style line and re-closing the bust dart, transferring the fitting to the new curved style line.

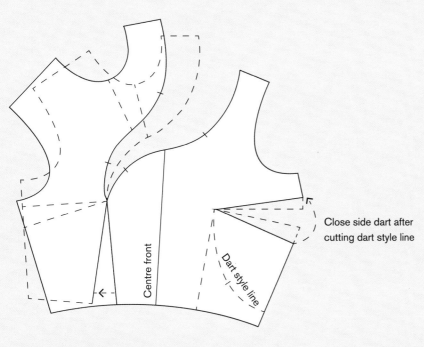

Close side dart after
cutting dart style line

Centre front

Dart style line

Prep pattern 2

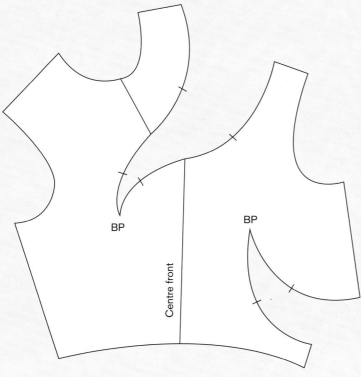

BP

BP

Centre front

Final pattern

42   **Pattern Fundamentals**

From 3D to 2D – basic blocks
Darts in design
Panel lines for fit and flare control
Complex style lines
Adding flare
Adding volume

TROUBLESHOOTING

In some designs, the dart does not appear to exist anywhere – it is not visible through darting or gathering. It is quite likely the garment is cut using a 'dartless block'. The block actually does have darts but they are spread around the body and not stitched in. The pattern example on page 43 shows where the darts go, and the problems that arise from not having a dart.

Problems
- Armhole can gape with a sleeveless garment.
- Fabric drags over the bust point.
- Too much fullness at the hem.
- Side seam becomes displaced, swinging forward or backward.

Solutions
- Cut fabric on the bias, the stretch in the bias will help to reduce drag.
- Use a fabric with a small percentage of stretch yarn.
- Sleeveless garments can be bound with edging or facing binding, which will shrink the curve, or cut facings slightly smaller (depends on fabric as to how much, approx 2–5mm).
- Realign the side seam by separating and rebalancing.

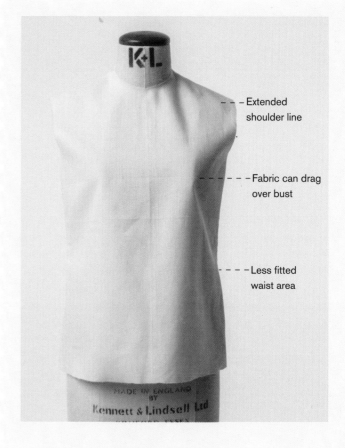

Extended shoulder line

Fabric can drag over bust

Less fitted waist area

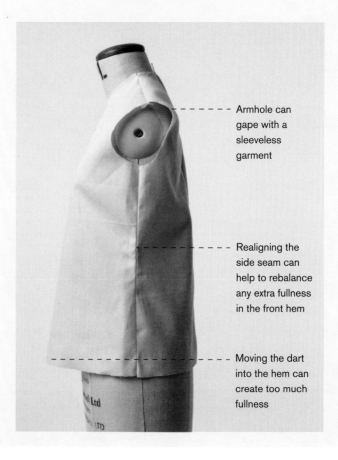

Armhole can gape with a sleeveless garment

Realigning the side seam can help to rebalance any extra fullness in the front hem

Moving the dart into the hem can create too much fullness

DARTLESS DESIGN

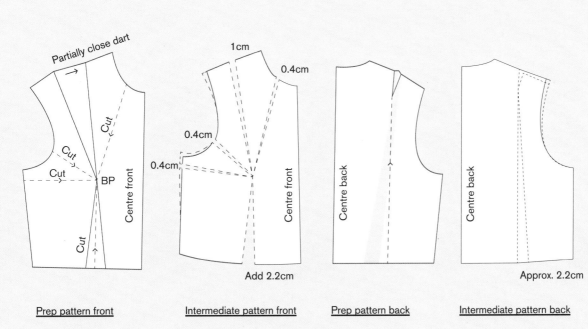

Partially close dart

Cut — Cut — Cut — Cut — BP — Centre front

1cm — 0.4cm

0.4cm — 0.4cm — Centre front

Add 2.2cm

Centre back — Centre back

Approx. 2.2cm

Prep pattern front — Intermediate pattern front — Prep pattern back — Intermediate pattern back

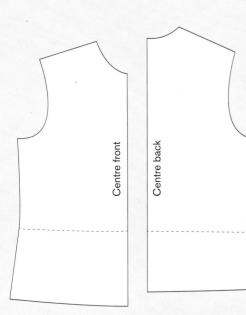

Centre front — Centre back

Final pattern front (extended to the hip) — Final pattern back (extended to the hip)

Step-by-step

FRONT

1.
Trace off front bodice block, draw lines radiating out from BP to neck, armhole, side seam and hem (waist) for moving the bust dart. Cut around pattern.

2.
Cut up new lines from outer edges to BP, being careful not to break them apart. Close shoulder dart, leaving 1cm in shoulder line. Spread cut lines open to introduce:
   0.4cm in neckline
   0.4cm in armhole
   0.4cm in side seam
with the remainder in the hem (approx 2.2cm or more). The dart is spread around the bust area and falls away at the hem.

3.
The shoulder line is now 1cm longer, but can be reduced 1cm by redrawing the armhole.

Note: The armhole will be longer so the sleeve will have less ease over the crown.

BACK

1.
Trace off back bodice block. Draw a line square to waist to touch the end of the shoulder dart.

2.
Cut up this line from the waist, fold some of the shoulder dart away enough to allow the cut line to open the waist the same as for the front (approx 2.2cm).

3.
Straighten the shoulder from NP (Neck Point). This raises the SP and makes the armhole bigger, so the sleeve has less ease over the crown. If it is too long the shoulder length can be reduced by redrawing the armhole, making sure it matches the front. The finished pattern example has been extended to the hip.

WHY DARTLESS?
Consider the design before cutting the pattern and ask the question 'why do I want a dartless garment? Does it enhance the design?' Perhaps the clean lines of the design would be broken, or a print may not look good cut up. Whatever the reason, think of ways to avoid dartless garments if you want it to be close-fitting. Remember you are enclosing the three-dimensional shape of the body with two-dimensional cloth.

44 **Pattern Fundamentals**   From 3D to 2D – basic blocks
Darts in design
Panel lines for fit and flare control
Complex style lines
Adding flare
Adding volume

PANEL LINES FOR FIT AND FLARE CONTROL

2

A basic block will give a limited range of shape and fitting possibilities, and in particular when fitting closely over, above and below the bust. Unless the fabric has a lot of stretch the pattern should be cut in such a way to give control over the body shape, and this is usually achieved by drawing 'style lines' where the fit is located. The style lines separate sections of the bodice (or elsewhere) and are referred to as 'panels'.

Panel lines (or any separated sections of a pattern) can also be used in design for colour and texture blocking and using different fabrics. Generally, the panels are cut following the same grain line as the block, but some allowance (up to 45 degrees) should still give good drape. The 1920s and 1930s used the behaviour of the bias grain and panels to create soft, body-skimming clothes.

Two examples of bodice panel lines are shown here. In the first, the panel lines pass through the BP and all of the bust and waist darts are incorporated in the panel (style) lines. In the second, the panel lines avoid the BP and the waist dart is incorporated but not the bust dart.

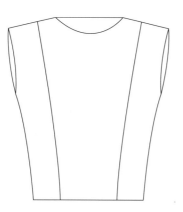

CENTRE SHOULDER TO WAIST PANELS
(Passing through BP)

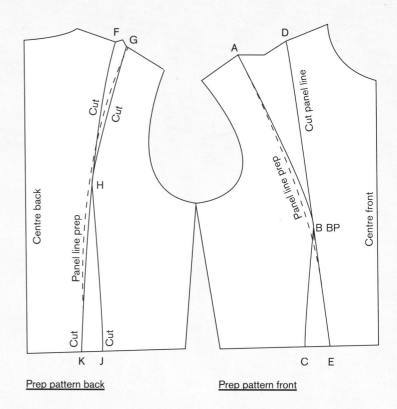

Prep pattern back   Prep pattern front

Step-by-step

1.
Prepare the back by tracing around the back bodice block to waist (or hip), marking all relevant darts and waistline. Check if the shoulder dart is exactly in the centre – if not, move it to the centre.

2.
Draw panel lines in gentle curves from either side of the central shoulder dart through the end of the dart and beyond, passing near the top end of the waist dart to the waist, leaving the width of the waist dart out, as in the front.

3.
Prepare the front by tracing around the front bodice block to the waist (or hip), marking all relevant darts and waistline.

4.
Draw a straight guide line from the CS (centre shoulder) to the BP (bust point). This will be the position the dart will be moved to. Cut along this line and close the bust dart away to move it to the CS position. If you begin with the bust dart in the centre shoulder position you will not need this step.

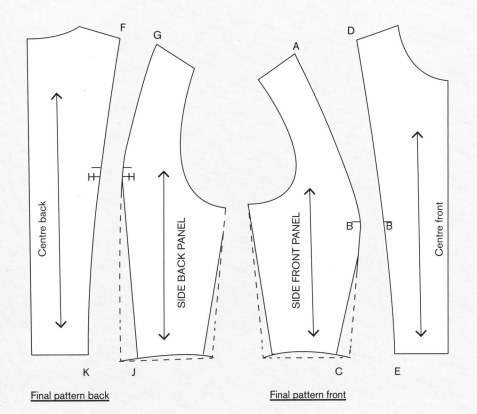

F G A D

Centre back

SIDE BACK PANEL

SIDE FRONT PANEL

Centre front

K J C E

Final pattern back   Final pattern front

B B

PANEL LINES

Always check that seams that are sewn together meet at right angles at the top and bottom of seam lines, and that they are the same length. Generally, this requires the adjoining lines to create right angles too.

5.

Mark balance points, measure the length of the lines and adjust if necessary. Draw grain lines square to waist or bias.

6.

Cut out and separate panels.

Note: The panels can be reduced at the waist and side seams for tighter fit.

7.

Place on another piece of paper and draw gentle curved lines from CS through BP to include the waist dart. You will be following the dart lines and removing the 'point' of the bust dart as it meets the waist dart at BP. Mark balance points at the BP. You will notice the line closer to the CF is flatter than the line towards the side seam. It is common to have one panel on a bodice sloping and fitting to a flatter one.

8.

Measure the lines that are being separated and adjust if needed so that they match. Mark the grain line square to the waist or bias. Cut along these new panel lines to separate the panels. The CF panel should be cut as a whole pattern piece if there is no opening.

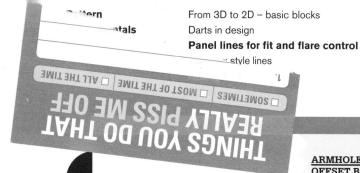

2

OFFSET PANEL LINES

This type of panel line needs to have some darts, because the line does not touch the BP. If it is quite close to BP the extra fullness can be eased in. The further the line is from the BP the greater the dart will show.

ARMHOLE TO WAIST – OFFSET BODICE PANEL LINES
(Not passing through BP)

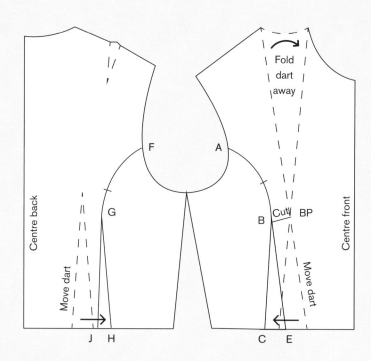

Prep pattern back   Prep pattern front

Step-by-step

1.
Prepare the back by tracing around the back bodice block to waist (or hip). Draw the 'lead' line which is closest to the CB line (F–G–J). If using a tailor's dummy, close the darts and pin onto the dummy so that you can see where you want to draw the panel lines. Use tape to mark out the line or draw with a soft pencil. In this example the panel line is in a curve from armhole to waist but away from the existing darts. Ignore the waist darts for now as they will move.

2.
Prepare the front by tracing around the front bodice block to waist (or hip), with bust dart in normal block position. Draw the 'lead' line which is closest to the CF line (A–B–C). If using a tailor's dummy close the darts and pin onto the dummy so that you can see where you want to draw the panel lines. Use tape to mark out the line or draw with a soft pencil. In this example the panel line is in a curve from armhole to waist but away from the BP. Ignore the waist darts for now as they will move.

Note: Keep bust dart closed whilst drawing the panel lines.

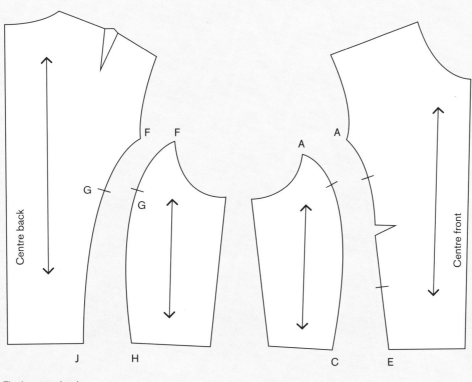

Final pattern back

Final pattern front

3.
Remove the back from the dummy, open pattern flat and tidy the rough 'lead' panel line. The armhole position of the back panel line does not need to match the level of the front, but it can be helpful for visual balance. Mark balance points.

4.
Draw the side panel line (F–G–H) with J–H measurement same as waist dart, measuring from the 'lead' panel line. Make sure the curved line is smooth.

5.
Measure these lines and adjust if they are not the same length. Cut along the panel lines and separate.

6.
Draw grain lines square to waist on all panels.

7.
Remove the front from the dummy, open pattern flat and tidy the rough lead panel line. If not using a dummy, draw flat to start and check against yourself. Draw a short line from BP to the panel line (B–BP). The bust dart will move in to this position. Mark at least two balance points along the panel line, one where the bust dart will meet this line.

8.
Draw the waist, shaping from the bust area so that the whole waist dart moves along the waistline, measuring from the 'lead' panel line. Make sure the curved line is smooth.

9.
Measure these lines and adjust if they are not the same length, then cut panel lines and separate.

10.
Cut along new dart line B–BP, close bust dart away.

48 **Pattern
Fundamentals**

From 3D to 2D – basic blocks
Darts in design
Panel lines for fit and flare control
Complex style lines
Adding flare
Adding volume

PANELS IN SKIRTS

2

Panels in skirts not only control shape and fit but also allow the hem width to be increased for a fuller hem line. The width can be added anywhere along the panel line so there are many 'looks' that can be achieved.

The number of panels that can be introduced depends on the design: a slim fitting but very full hem will need around eight panels overall, but it is possible to have more (within reason). Front and back generally have equal numbers of panels and are of equal size and shape, but if the design requires, for example, more fullness at the back so that the back kicks out below the buttocks, then different panel patterns will be needed.

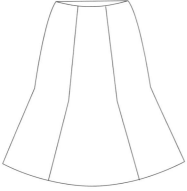

SIMPLE FLARED SIX-PANEL SKIRT

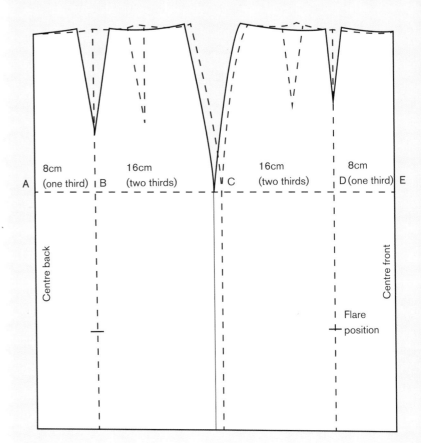

Prep pattern back

Step-by-step

Note: Measurements for the example are in brackets.

1.
Prepare by placing the front and back skirt blocks together so that the side seams touch and the hemline is square. Trace around the blocks marking all relevant darts, hip and side seam.

2.
Balance the front and back equally, marking a halfway point along the hip line (24cm). This moves the front side seam towards the back (1cm), and reduces the width of the back. Draw the new side seams following the original curves. Square down to the hemline.

3.
Draw panel lines dividing the hip width into one-third proportions. As the CF and CB are on the fold, calculate one third to centre panels (8cm) and two thirds to the side seams (16cm). This will give three panels in the front and three in the back.

4.
Move the waist darts to the panel lines so that they are equally distributed either side. The shaping at the back will be greater than the front. Redraw the waistline with the new dart positions, that is, make sure the length of the dart is equal both sides. Adjust if necessary.

LEVELLING THE HEM

Measure the length of the straight line to hem and use the tape measure to swing out to the extra width point and mark the new hemline position. It will rise upwards depending on the amount of flare added. Gently curve the angle where the lines meet so that there are no corners.

ADDING MORE PANELS

If more hem width or shape control is needed then eight or even 16 panels can be cut. The preparation is the same, equalizing the side seams and transferring the darts into the panel lines. The waist darts are distributed equally between panel lines for front and back. An eight-panel skirt will have a CF seam.

HEM WIDTH

It is important to not extend the hem width beyond its useful purpose, for example having three panels and adding too much width at the hem will only result in the extra flare folding over. This may be, however, a look that the design needs, so all things need to be considered. Experimenting with different numbers of panels and widths will help you to understand the possibilities.

Y
Z
Side front panel
Centre front line
Side front panel
Add 6   Add 6 Add 6   Add 6 Add 6   Add 6
R   S
Final pattern front

Y
29cm
Z
Side back panel
Centre back line
Side back panel
Add 6   Add 6 Add 6   Add 6 Add 6   Add 6
R   S
Final pattern back

5.
Mark the level on each panel where the flare will begin (29cm from waist here, but this will depend on the design). Mark balance points on side seams and dart ends, and label each section before cutting and separating the panels.

6.
Place the panels on paper so that there is space to extend either side at the hem for extra width, flare (6cm plus seam allowance). Draw a line from the flare point at the hem (6cm) up to meet the start point on the existing panel line. Do this for every panel section.

7.
Draw new hemlines for each section, making sure they meet the side seam at right angles. (Total hem width for this example is 84cm.)

From 3D to 2D – basic blocks
Darts in design
Panel lines for fit and flare control
Complex style lines
Adding flare
Adding volume

COMPLEX STYLE LINES

2

Style lines on a garment combine features of panel lines, yokes and shaping with or without darts. They can also be used to control fit, flare, volume and other design details such as colour blocking or seam finishes. It is the design that will determine where lines are, and from which particular shape they may start with.

The possibilities of style lines are endless, but beware when designing of drawing just outlines and filling in with lines. Think of overall shape and in 3D: front, side and back.

The example here can be used for colour blocking, changing textures, or highlighting seams. The waist darts are folded away and move in to the seam line of the yokes, and therefore the upper style lines are fairly determined by the length of the darts.

REMOVING THE SIDE SEAM

The lower style lines curve front to back and eliminate the side seam so it is cut in one.

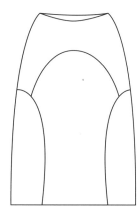

COMPLEX STYLE LINES

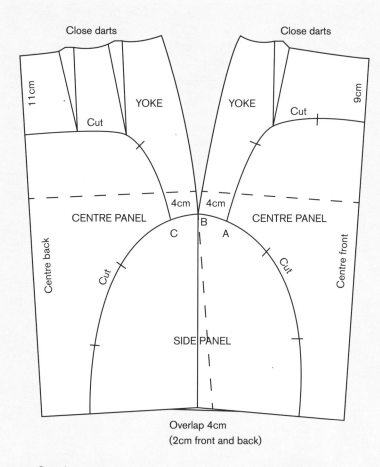

Close darts   Close darts

11 cm   YOKE   YOKE   9cm

Cut   Cut

4cm   4cm

CENTRE PANEL   CENTRE PANEL

Centre back   C   B   A   Centre front

Cut   Cut

SIDE PANEL

Overlap 4cm
(2cm front and back)

Complete pattern

Step-by-step

1.
Prepare by placing the side seams together and then reducing the width at the hem (4cm) by overlapping one over the other (2cm). Trace round, marking all relevant darts and hip line.

2.
Mark style lines using cotton tape, removable tape or a soft pencil. It is useful to use a dummy as you will see the lines in 3D.

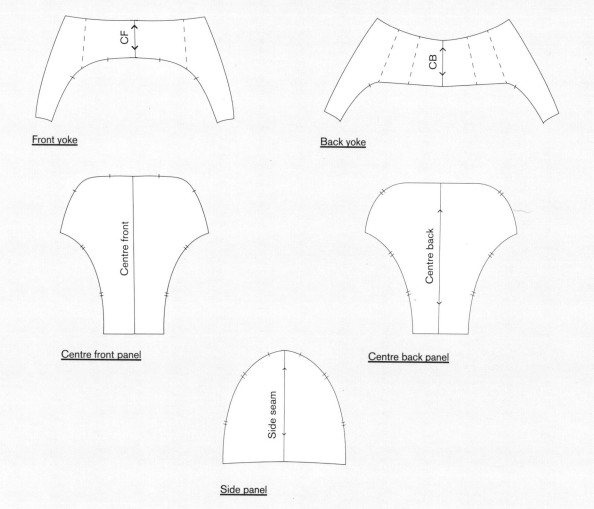

Front yoke

Back yoke

Centre front

Centre front panel

Centre back

Centre back panel

Side seam

Side panel

DRAWING STYLE LINES

It is helpful to use a tailor's dummy when deciding on style lines because working in 3D provides a real view of how they will behave on the body and it is easier to stand back and check the proportions and shapes. Use narrow tape or removable tape, or a soft pencil (not normally recommended for pattern cutting but good for marking a line without applying too much pressure on the paper). If a dummy is not available, draw soft lines and check against yourself in a mirror, or on someone else.

TROUBLESHOOTING

When assembling the garment, there are convex and concave curves coming together. Snipping the concave curve just to the stitch line will release it and make it easier to sew.

3.
Side panel: Draw a curved panel front to back, you can copy one side to the other for balance. The side seam curve meets the hem at right angles.

4.
Yokes: Draw the front yoke with the waist dart closed and the yoke style line passing through the end of the dart and down to the side panel line A–B = 4cm width.

Draw the back yoke similar to the front, adjusting the darts to meet the yoke line and down to the side panel B–C = 4cm width.

Mark balance points on all style lines then cut and separate each section.

5.
Final pattern, yokes: Close away the darts and redraw the yoke panels on the fold of the paper so that they are whole pieces. Check that the style lines meet the CF and CB at right angles and the lines are smooth.

6.
Centre panels: Redraw with CF and CB on fold of paper so that panels are whole pieces.

7.
Side panels: The side seam is joined, but find the grain by folding in half and using the crease line. Adjust the slight curve at the hemline where the seams have overlapped.

Measurements for this example:
Front yoke: CF depth 9cm, width at side 4cm
Back yoke: CB depth 11cm, width at side 4cm
Centre panel: 26cm from waist at side seam, width across at hem 30.5cm.

From 3D to 2D – basic blocks
Darts in design
Panel lines for fit and flare control
Complex style lines
Adding flare
Adding volume

ADDING FLARE

2

The most common method of adding flare or extra fullness to a pattern is called 'slash and spread'. Decide on where flare is wanted in the basic block and how much. There are several considerations when adding flare.

- **Fabric type** – thickness and weight – thick fabric will hold the shape and therefore the amount of flare added will be visible. A thin fabric can take a lot of flare as it will drop into folds at the hem.
- **Uniformity of flare** – Spread the flare equally around the shape – normally it is not just added to the sides because of the change of grain line. Balance front and back additional flare width inset equally, but front and back overall hem width may not be the same.
- **Grain line** – If a pattern becomes very flared it will need to be divided into sections (panels) so that each section (panel) has the same grain line. The number of sections (panels) depends on how much flare is in the design. This is explored in chapter 4.

SIMPLE SLASH AND SPREAD METHOD ADDING FLARE TO A SKIRT BLOCK

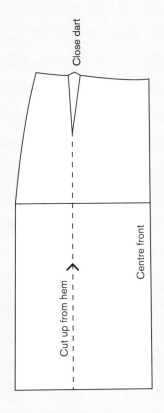

Prep pattern front

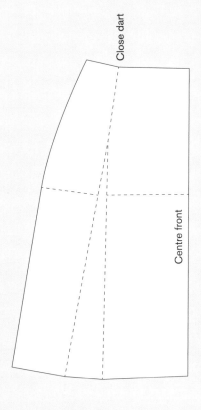

Final pattern front

This method uses the redistribution of waist darts to add flare to the hem.

Step-by-step

FRONT

1.
Prepare by tracing around the front skirt block and marking all relevant dart and hip lines. Decide on the length of the skirt and adjust hem length. It is best to measure a length from the waist down the side of the body. Cut around block.

2.
Draw a line square to the hemline through the end of the dart point.

3.
Cut up this line from the hem to the end of the dart, close the waist dart away so that the hem opens and adds width.

4.
Measure the width that has been added into the hem.

Note: For a wider hem slash all the way to the waist, close the dart and open the hem to the desired width, taking care to pay attention to the principles of grain line, hem width and fabric type.

5.
Complete pattern by drawing smooth curves at waistline and hemline.

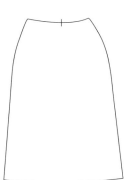

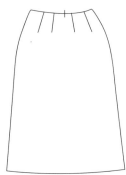

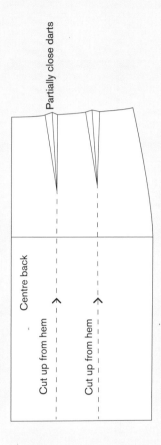

Partially close darts

Centre back

Cut up from hem

Cut up from hem

Prep pattern back

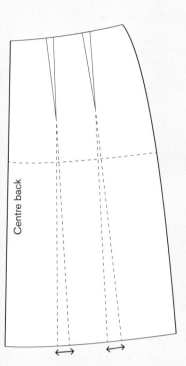

Centre back

Open same width as front

Final pattern back

Step-by-step

BACK

1.
Prepare by tracing around the back basic skirt block, marking all dart and hip lines. Adjust the hem length to match the front pattern at sides. Cut around block.

2.
Square two lines from the hem through the dart's end point to the waist. These will be the slash lines.

3.
Cut up from the hem to the end of the dart points, open each section equally to match the front width addition measurement. Fold away the darts enough to allow for equal amounts to be added at the hem. There will be small darts left because the back darts are greater than the front.

Note: For a wider hem follow the front instructions. Make sure the hem insert widths are balanced.

4.
Complete pattern by drawing smooth curves at the waistline and hemline.

From 3D to 2D – basic blocks

Darts in design

Panel lines for fit and flare control

Complex style lines

Adding flare

Adding volume

2

CONTROLLING HIP FLARE WITH A YOKE

This allows the waist and hip to fit by separating the fitted section and flared section.

DARTS

Darts must always be closed when drawing yokes or separations around the upper skirt area.

YOKES

Yokes usually allow the waist darts to be moved from their original position to a yoke line.

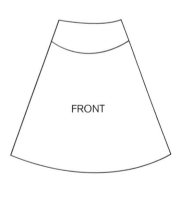

FRONT

BACK

YOKED FLARED SKIRT

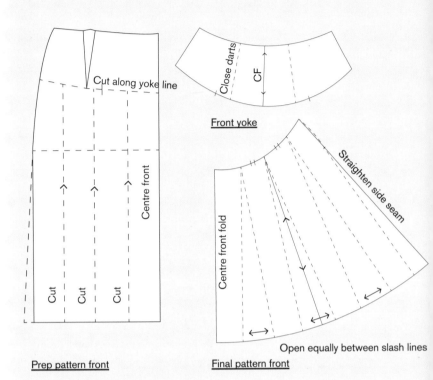

Prep pattern front

Final pattern front

Cut along yoke line

Centre front

Cut Cut Cut

Close darts

CF

Front yoke

Centre front fold

Straighten side seam

Open equally between slash lines

Step-by-step

FRONT

1.
Prepare by tracing around the front skirt block, marking all relevant information.

2.
Yoke: Fold the darts away at the waist and draw or mark with tape a yoke line across the skirt from SS (side seam) to CF. In this example the line dips down and crosses through the end of the dart (using a tailor's dummy helps to see lines across 3D). Neaten line when laid flat but keep the darts closed. Mark at least one balance mark on this line.

3.
Lower skirt: Below the yoke draw evenly spaced slash lines from hem to yoke and square to the hip line.

4.
Cut along the yoke line and separate the top from the bottom.

5.
Adding flare to the skirt: Cut up from the hem along the slash lines to just the edge of the yoke line – do not cut off but get as close to the edge as possible. Spread the sections apart and add equal amounts of flare between each section. The amount of flare will vary depending on the look. Straighten the side seam by extending from the hip, this adds more flare to the pattern (this can be done at the preparation stage).

6.
Retrace the skirt, making good all lines. Retrace the yoke with CF on fold of paper for a whole pattern. Mark grain line through the centre of the pattern.

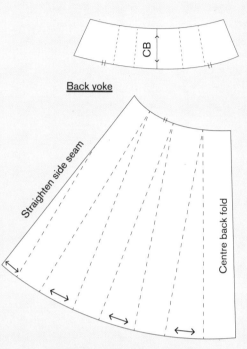

Back yoke

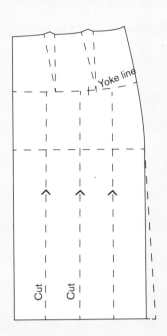

Yoke line

Cut Cut

Straighten side seam

Centre back fold

CB

Open equally between slash lines

Prep pattern back

Final pattern back

Step-by-step

BACK

1.
Prepare by tracing around the back skirt block, marking all relevant information.

2.
Yoke: Fold the darts away at the waist and draw or mark with tape a yoke line across the skirt from SS to CB. In this example the line dips down and crosses through the end of the darts (using a tailor's dummy helps to see lines across 3D). Neaten line when laid flat but keep the darts closed.

Important: check the front and back yokes are the same depth from the waist at the SS. The CB yoke may be lower in the back than front.

Mark balance points at intervals along the yoke line – it helps to differentiate the front from the back if they are spaced and marked differently, perhaps having two sets for the back.

3.
Lower skirt: Below the yoke, draw evenly spaced slash lines from hem to yoke and square to the hip line.

4.
Trace new skirt pattern, drawing good curves at yoke seam and hem and transferring all relevant pattern information including grain line.

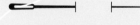

TROUBLESHOOTING

The back and front skirt may not be the same width but will have the same balance of flare.

56   **Pattern
Fundamentals**

From 3D to 2D – basic blocks
Darts in design
Panel lines for fit and flare control
Complex style lines
Adding flare
Adding volume

ADDING VOLUME

2

Creating volume in a shape can be achieved with the 'slash and spread' method. If the volume is in a specific area or part of the garment, it should be directed there only, if it is equally distributed around the body then the volume is added throughout. It is generally considered that if a garment has volume it is gathered or pleated into a smaller part at some point. How much volume is determined by the following:

- the design
- the fabric
- where it is on the body

PEG-TOP SKIRT

In this example, the volume is introduced into the waist, and to accentuate the sense of volume, the hem width is introduced. Variations of this method can be explored by introducing yokes or separations, or used for adding volume to a sleeve from a lower seam line, for example.

WAIST CURVE

Finish pattern by retracing the shape and adjusting the curve of the waist – this will cut off some excess. Curve hem and check CF and side seams are squared as they meet these lines.

PEG-TOP SKIRT

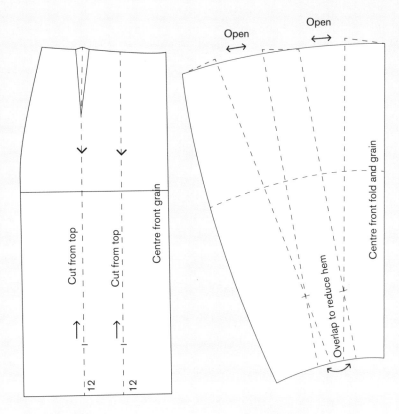

Prep pattern front

Final pattern front

Step-by-step

FRONT

1.
Prepare by tracing around the basic front skirt block to the desired length, marking all relevant information.

2.
Draw two slash lines square to the hemline up through the centre of the waist dart to the waist, and another about 6cm toward the CF line. Mark a position about 12cm up from the hemline, depending on the length of the skirt. This point will be where the line will fold away to the hem, creating a dart as the upper section opens out.

3.
Slash down both lines from the waist to the point marked on the slash line, open out the waist equally for each section. The amount depends on the look, cloth and position on the body.

4.
Below the end of the slash point, fold away into darts so that the hem is reduced (ensure there is still enough hem for walking). Alternatively, use the dart reduction at the hem as a control of the upper volume. Whatever you close away into the dart affects the size of the opening above and so, consequently, the volume.

5.
Finish the pattern by retracing the shape and adjusting the curve of the waist – this will level off the edges. Curve the hem and check CF and side seams are squared as they meet these lines. Place pattern on fold of paper to create a full pattern.

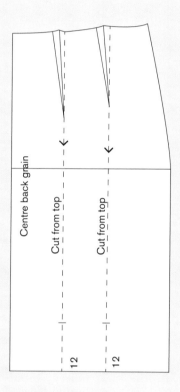

Prep pattern back

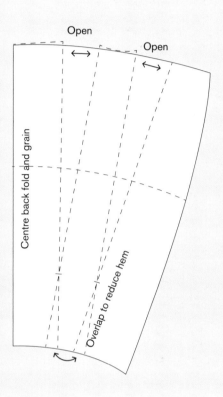

Final pattern back

Step-by-step

BACK

1.
Prepare by tracing around
the back basic skirt block
and marking all relevant
information.

2.
Draw in two slash lines
squared from the hemline
through the dart points to the
waist. Mark a point 12cm up
from the hemline to where the
slash will end.

3.
Follow the steps for the front
so that equal volume is added
between slashed lines at
the waist.

4.
Finish pattern by tracing and
correcting lines as for the
front. Place on fold of paper
for a full pattern.

58   **Pattern Fundamentals**   From 3D to 2D – basic blocks
Darts in design
Panel lines for fit and flare control
Complex style lines
Adding flare
Adding volume

2

ADDING VOLUME TO A HEM

Bishop sleeve

In this example, volume is added to the lower part of the pattern, the hem. To show how slash and spread works for a sleeve as well as a skirt or top, the sleeve has fullness at the wrist (hem) and not at the crown (sleeve head). The method could be reversed (as for the peg-top skirt) so that there is volume in the crown and none at the wrist (hem).

Volume and length must be decided before the pattern begins, so make a test sample. How the sleeve will be finished, e.g. elastic, binding, or cuff – all these will affect the length. If a long cuff is wanted then reduce the length of the sleeve by 2 or 3cm less than the cuff.

BISHOP SLEEVE

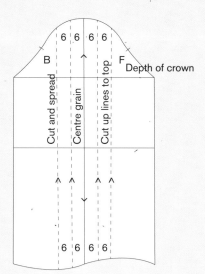

Prep pattern

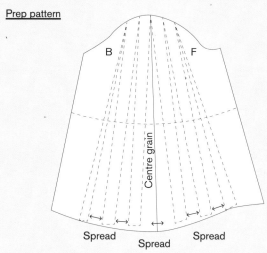

Final pattern

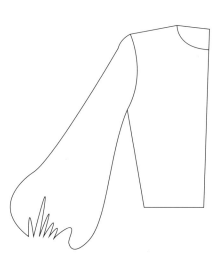

Step-by-step

1.
Prepare by tracing around the whole sleeve basic block, marking in depth of crown line, centre line and back sleeve opening.

2.
Draw four parallel slash lines square to depth of crown line, two either side of the centre line approximately 6cm apart.

3.
Cut/slash up these lines and the centre line from hem to crown, but do not cut right off.

4.
Spread each section, adding more in the centre and less toward the sides, equally so that the fullness is balanced. Test how much you need (see opposite), but often gathers need twice the finished length.

5.
Adjust for a cuff by reducing the length by cuff depth, and then add 'overhang' on centre line approximately 1–3cm.

SHORT PUFFED SLEEVE

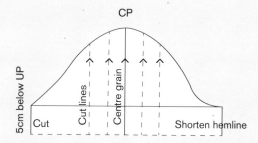

Prep pattern

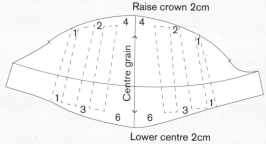

Final pattern

Step-by-step

1.
Trace around basic sleeve block to a desired length (in this case it is 5cm below underarm). Draw in centre line and depth of crown line – this helps to keep control of the shape when separating sections.

2.
Draw equally spaced slash lines (approximately 6cm) squared to the hem to the crown of the sleeve. The centre line is also used as a slash line.

3.
Cut around the sleeve, cut slash lines and separate all sections.

4.
On another piece of paper draw a new centre line and square a line across approximate depth of crown as a guideline.

Carefully lay the cut sections onto paper and mark with a centre line, using the depth of crown line as a guide to keep the sections level.

Spread each crown section equally either side of the centre line 4cm, then 2cm, then 1cm away from the centre toward the side.

5.
Keeping this new top sleeve steady, spread the hem sections out wider so that the lower ratio becomes 6cm, then 3cm, then 1cm. You will notice that this affects the top shape and the sleeve head is uneven. Pin and secure the pattern.

6.
Add extra length for volume at the crown and the hem of the sleeve. Raise the crown at the centre by 2cm (or more depending on look and fabric). Lower the hem at the centre by 2cm (or more as above). Complete the crown lines and hemlines in smooth curves.

ADDING VOLUME TOP AND BOTTOM

Short puffed sleeve

In this example, volume is added to the top and bottom of the pattern with the 'slash and spread' method. It also shows what happens to a pattern when there is a difference in the amount of volume added between one area and another. It also introduces adding extra height or length to a pattern for a more voluminous or puffy look.

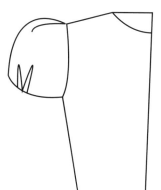

FINISHING
Decisions about how the sleeve will be finished, either elasticated, with a cuff, binding or other finish, must be considered in the length.

HOW MUCH VOLUME?
Test the amount of volume you want by gathering or pleating a length of measured material, consider how it looks and make adjustments of more or less. Measure the gathered length of this section, so that when opened out again it can be established how much volume per measure is added.

Shape

This chapter looks at how pattern cutting can affect the overall silhouette, shape and fit of the garment. Understanding how shape will determine the overall outcome of the garment design is an essential skill. Here, we will look in particular at how linear, inverted triangle, square, trapeze, hourglass, dome, lantern, cocoon and balloon shapes can be created.

62 Shape in design
64 Linear
68 Inverted triangle
72 Square
78 Trapeze
82 Hourglass
88 Dome
94 Lantern
98 Cocoon
102 Balloon

62   Shape   **Shape in design**
Linear
Inverted triangle
Square
Trapeze

Hourglass
Dome
Lantern
Cocoon
Balloon

SHAPE IN DESIGN

Fashion design is design for the body. The body will carry the design, and the garment will reveal the curves of the body, or use the body to support its structure.

Fashion design embodies design principles of which shape is an essential ingredient. It is commonly referred to as the 'silhouette', but a garment can be made up of more than one shape so this book prefers to use the terminology of shape.

Fashion shapes (and proportions) are linked to cultural and social change, and represent some aspect of these changes. The 'linear' shape of the early twentieth century was a freedom from corseted, tight garments; the body was liberated from fussy and controlling clothing. It represented modernism, clean lines, limited surface decoration, and was symbolic of women's liberation. Similarly, it was the shape of the 1960s, a time of space travel and futuristic thinking; youth culture had emerged and the childlike 'shift' dress dominated fashion. In the 1990s, the shape was referred to as 'minimalist', taken to its very essence of simplicity.

Exaggerated shapes tend to have some link with extreme or specific situations, for example, the famous 'hourglass' shape of Dior's post-war suit, ignoring fabric rationing, used up to 15 yards of cloth to create an accentuated hip and full skirt from a tight-fitting bodice. The austere war years and limited fabric supplies were defined by this design statement, along with the psychological factor of what the physical indication of full hips may imply. After the war a nation needed to be repopulated, and after years of masculine work and dressing in rough fabric with masculine shapes, women were ready for a 'feminine' shape.

Another example was seen in the 1980s when women rose into the male-dominated corporate world and started to wear fashion shapes that extended the shoulder line, sending a message of 'power'. These shapes mimicked men's wide shoulders and went even further in exaggerating them. Power was also embodied through actual body shape and exercise, celebrating this fitness in tight-fitting clothes that revealed the toned body.

Interestingly, during the 1940s similar shape trends had already emerged. Women had suddenly had to take on men's work and found themselves wearing suits and uniforms. Again, a use of squared shoulders in all spheres of fashion mimicked men's tailoring. However, this was never as extreme as the 1980s as women were not expressing a desire to enter a man's world of work, they were already in it.

Shape has many cultural and historical references and this book draws upon this to develop fashion design.

Shape is an important starting point for creating patterns; it informs a great deal about the design intention. This book uses shape as part of a sequence: design, shape, fit and detail. Ultimately, everything can be reduced to a shape, and this can help to consider proportions and balance, which can take years to refine as a designer and pattern cutter.

This chapter demonstrates methods to create the most common shapes, and links to other chapters.

Alexandre Herchovita

I am too emotional sometimes, but I rationally think about the shape.

Opposite
Shapes on the catwalk
The nine shapes covered in this chapter:

Top row left to right:
Prada SS10 (trapeze)
Louis Vuitton AW09 (balloon)
Donna Karan AW10 (cocoon)

Middle row left to right:
Chapurin SS11 (dome)
Gareth Pugh SS12 (hourglass)
Tse Goh, Central Saint Martins MA Graduate Show 2010 (inverted triangle)

Bottom row left to right:
Nicole Farhi SS12 (lantern)
Manish Arora AW07 (linear)
Emilio de la Morena AW09 (square)

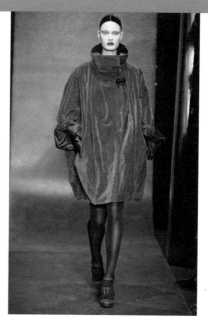

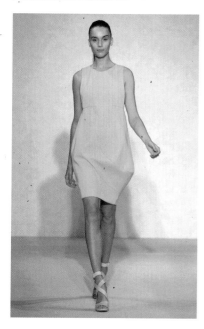

64 **Shape**

Shape in design
Linear
Inverted triangle
Square
Trapeze

Hourglass
Dome
Lantern
Cocoon
Balloon

LINEAR

3

This simple linear shape is the most iconic and widely used shape. It is also referred to as 'A-line'. The shape is the foundation for many garment designs, particularly shift dresses and tops. It was the shape of the 1960's Mary Quant mini dress, and is still popular in many designer collections. The linear shape can be virtually straight, but generally the hem is wider as this is visually more satisfying because of perspective reducing the visual width as we look down toward the hem. It is also the basis for a wider hem shape, such as the trapeze.

View magazine
A celebration of the everyday...

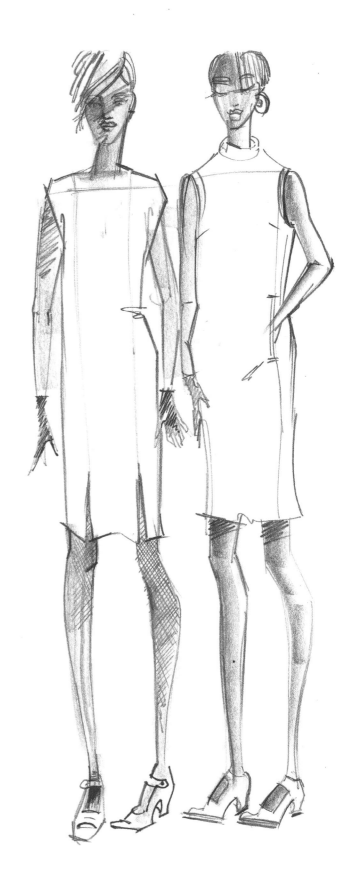

Shape in design	Hourglass
Linear	Dome
Inverted triangle	Lantern
Square	Cocoon
Trapeze	Balloon

3

CREATING THE LINEAR SHAPE

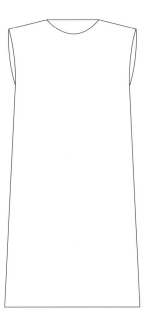

Raise up 1cm

Close dart to open hem

BP

Cut along slash line ↑

CF grain

Add 1cm hem width

Reduce width 1cm

BP

Straighten side seam

CF grain

3cm

Prep pattern front   Final pattern front

Step-by-step

FRONT

1.
Trace off front bodice block and move bust dart to the side seam, extending beyond the hips to the required hem length. Mark in all relevant information.

2.
Draw a slash line squared from the hem to the BP. Cut up this line to BP and partially close the bust dart to introduce 3cm into the hemline (the more you close the dart the more the hem will open).

3.
Side seam: Raise the UP (underarm point) at least 1cm and reduce width 1cm or more depending on fit. Temporarily close the bust dart. Draw a straight new side seam line from the new underarm position to a point at least 1cm (or more) wider at the hem, taking the line through hip point.

4.
Redraw new armhole and retrace whole pattern with a curved hemline. Trace through closed dart before opening pattern.

5.
Reduce the length of the bust dart 5cm away from BP. Fold this new dart closed and trace through along the side seam. This dart is shorter as bust darts are rarely stitched to BP.

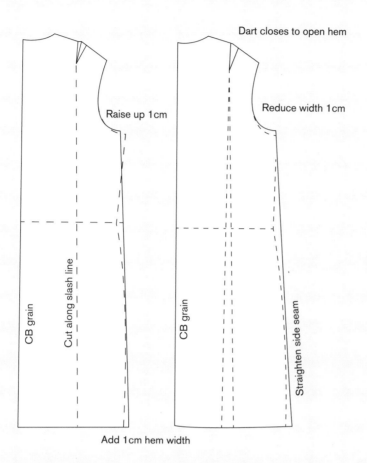

Dart closes to open hem

Raise up 1cm

Reduce width 1cm

CB grain

Cut along slash line

CB grain

Straighten side seam

Add 1cm hem width

Prep pattern back

Final pattern back

BACK

1.
Trace off back bodice block, extending beyond the hip to match the front length. Mark all relevant information.

2.
Draw a slash line squared from hem to end of shoulder dart.

3.
Adjust underarm width and height as front. Draw a straight new side seam from this point through the hip point to point 1cm (or more) at hemline, to match front. Draw new curved armhole.

4.
Cut up slash line to dart end, close dart very slightly to open the hem 3cm (or more). This will reduce the shoulder dart.

5.
Complete pattern by redrawing the whole new shape.

Shape in design	Hourglass
Linear	Dome
Inverted triangle	Lantern
Square	Cocoon
Trapeze	Balloon

INVERTED TRIANGLE

3

This shape can be used in many ways, as a simple shoulder extension to a more complex structured shape. It has been popular in the 1980s, 1990s and through the 2000s, appearing in many different guises. The shape can look quite different depending on the fabric, the toile examples on page 68 are made in bamboo silk, which gives a more solid silhouette and silk jersey, which drapes over the arms. It is worth experimenting with different fabrics to understand what this shape can do.

View magazine
Upturned balance is maintained by keeping things slim through the hips and narrowing hemlines.

3

CREATING THE INVERTED TRIANGLE SHAPE

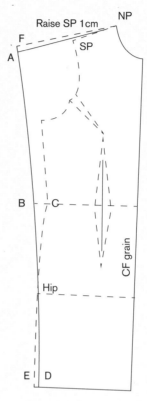

Prep pattern front

NP–A = 27cm

B–C = 3cm

E–D = 1cm

A–F = 1.5cm

Final pattern front

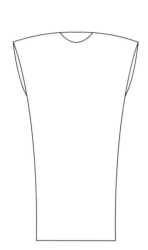

Silk jersey

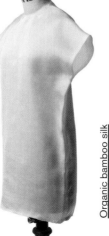

Organic bamboo silk

Step-by-step

FRONT

1.

Prepare by tracing around the bodice block with the dart in the armhole position, extending beyond the hip line to the hem length. Draw a hemline square to the CF. Mark all relevant darts, waist and hip lines.

Note: If starting with the basic block, move the dart into the armhole position first.

2.

Shoulder line: Raise SP 1cm and draw a temporary extended new shoulder line NP–F (27cm). Point A is 1.5cm below F, squared to line NP–F. Draw finished shoulder NP–A in a gentle curved line, passing through raised SP.

3.

Side seam: Mark points B–C 3cm beyond waist and E–D 1cm in at hemline. Draw a gently curving line squared from the new extended shoulder line towards the waist, hip and hemline, passing through B, touching the hip line to D. Keep the line straight from hip to D.

4.

Mark new underarm, waist and hip points on this new line.

5.

Finish pattern by retracing the whole pattern.

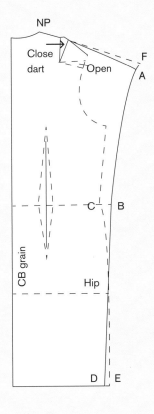

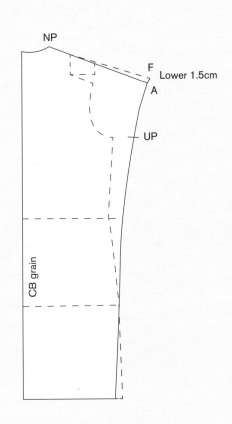

Prep pattern back

NP–A = 27cm

B–C = 3cm

E–D = 1cm

A–F = 1.5cm

Final pattern back

Step-by-step

BACK

1.

Prepare by tracing around the back bodice block, extending beyond the hip line to the hem length to match the front length. Mark all relevant darts, waist and hip lines. Square the hemline to the CB line.

2.

Shoulder line: Move the shoulder dart into the armhole, this raises the SP 1.5cm to match the front.

3.

Draw a temporary new shoulder line NP–F (27cm). Point A is 1.5cm below F, squared to line NP–F. Draw finished shoulder NP–A in a gentle curved line passing through raised SP.

4.

Side seam: Mark points B–C 3cm beyond waist and E–D 1cm in at hemline. Draw a gently curving line squared from the new extended shoulder line towards the waist, hip and hemline, passing through B and touching the hip line to D. Keep the line straight from hip to D.

5.

Finish pattern by retracing the whole pattern, marking underarm, waist and hip points on the new side seam.

72   **Shape**

Shape in design
Linear
Inverted triangle
Square
Trapeze

Hourglass
Dome
Lantern
Cocoon
Balloon

SQUARE

3

Although described as a 'square shape', the pattern for a square garment would actually be a rectangle, as the length is greater than the width. This shape is also known as the kaftan, and was popular in the 1970s when the trend was for hippy fashion inspired by peasant costume. Usually, the shape is more refined than the example – the shoulder line is sloped and fabric under the arm is reduced. The big loose shape without darts and no formal side seams can be successful in soft fabrics that will float around the body, such as chiffon and silk crepe, or fabrics that hang with some weight, such as some jersey fabrics. When the shoulder sloping and reduction of volume under the arm continues then it would become a dolman or batwing sleeve. These types of patterns are defined as 'grown on', meaning that the sleeve has been cut as part of the bodice pattern.

The Exhibition, London 2010
The shoulder is an important element in the Maison Martin Margiela silhouette.

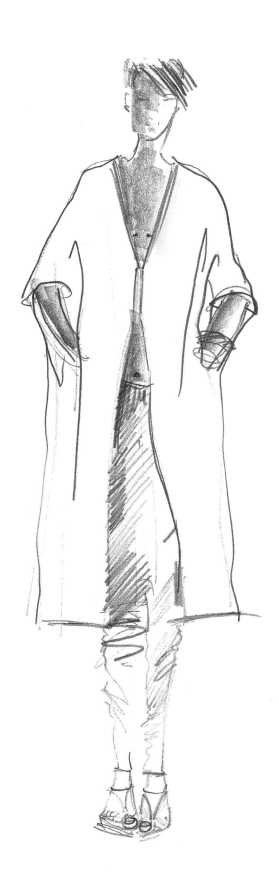

Shape in design   Hourglass
Linear   Dome
Inverted triangle   Lantern
Square   Cocoon
Trapeze   Balloon

3

CREATING THE SQUARE SHAPE

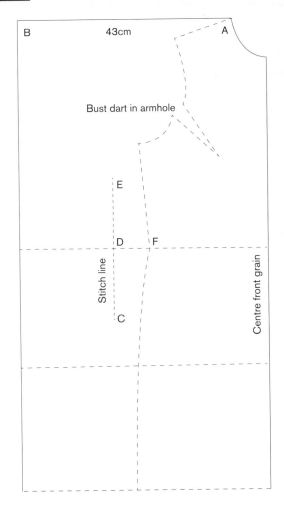

B   43cm   A

Bust dart in armhole

E

D   F

Stitch line

C

Centre front grain

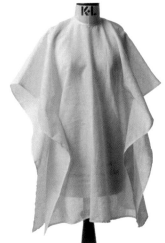

<u>Final pattern front</u>
A–B = 43cm
C–D = 15cm
D–E = 10cm
F–D = 10cm

Step-by-step

FRONT

1.
Allowing for extra width, trace around the front bodice block marking in the waist and hip lines. Extend length to required hem length (24cm below waist). The bust dart must be moved to armhole position so it does not interfere with any measurements, but does not need to be marked onto the pattern as it will not be stitched away.

2.
Square a line across from the extended CF line through the NP (neck point) the length required (43cm) or to the elbow level of the sleeve. Mark SP (shoulder point).

3.
Square the side of the pattern to the shoulder line down to the hemline. Square back to the CF line.

4.
Mark a point along the extended waistline where the sides will be joined (10cm). This allows width at the side. Finish pattern by marking stitching lines above (10cm) and below (15cm) the waistline from this point.

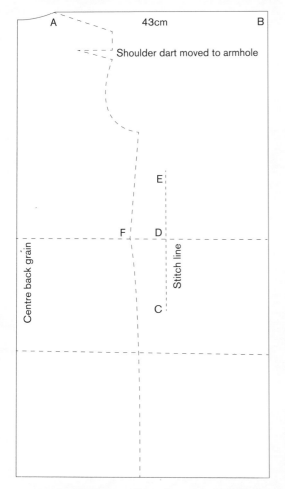

A   43cm   B

Shoulder dart moved to armhole

E

F   D

Stitch line

Centre back grain

C

Final pattern back

A–B = 43cm

C–D = 15cm

D–E = 10cm

F–D = 10cm

TROUBLESHOOTING

Before you start, calculate how much paper you'll need to draft this pattern, as it extends beyond the block pattern to include the length of the sleeve.

Step-by-step

BACK

1.
Allowing for extra width, trace around the back bodice block marking in the waist, hip and shoulder dart. At this stage move the shoulder dart to the armhole. Extend length to required hem length (24cm below waist).

2.
Square a line across from the extended CB line through the NP (neck point) to the length required (43cm) or to the elbow level of the sleeve. Mark SP (shoulder point).

3.
Square the side of the pattern to the shoulder line down to the hemline. Square back to the CB line.

4.
Mark a point along the extended waistline where the sides will be joined (10cm). This allows width at the side. Finish pattern by marking stitching lines above (10cm) and below (15cm) the waistline from this point.

[Case study]
ZOE HARCUS

Zoe's collection was inspired by flatpack boxes, and the turned back sections that create the boxes when folded up.

The strong boxy shape of the squared shoulders shows that squared shapes can be interpreted in many ways. The extended shoulders are defined by folds where the angle changes, and there is an upper and under sleeve section which allows the shoulder to extend to the sleeve. The complex pattern and construction creates a simple square silhouette.

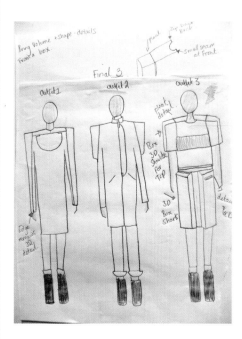

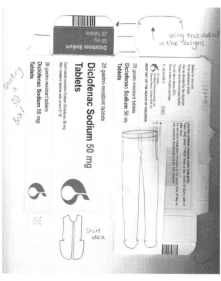

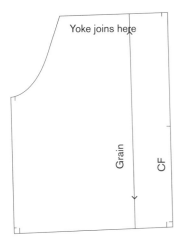

Front body

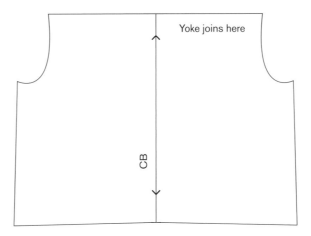

Back body

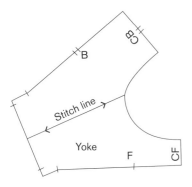

Front and back are joined at the shoulder to form a front-to-back yoke. The top sleeve is joined on lines F and B.

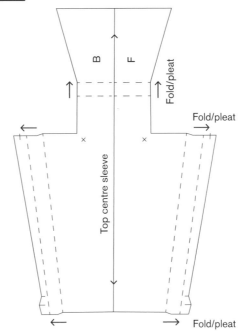

The top sleeve has pleats and is joined to the yoke on matching lines F and B.

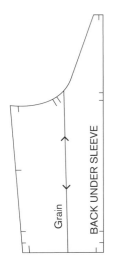

Under sleeve sections are joined to the body and top sleeve.

TRAPEZE

3

The trapeze shape is a wider linear or A-line shape, with controlled fullness added where it is needed. The fabric will determine how much flare can be added.

Stefano Pilati
Because it is Yves Saint Laurent, I think about the silhouette.

Shape in design	Hourglass
Linear	Dome
Inverted triangle	Lantern
Square	Cocoon
Trapeze	Balloon

3

CREATING THE TRAPEZE SHAPE

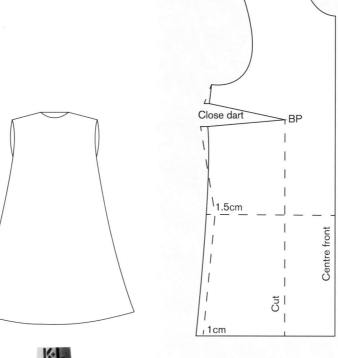

Prep pattern front   Intermediate pattern front

Step-by-step

FRONT

1.
Prepare by tracing around the bodice block with the bust dart in the side seam, marking in all relevant darts, waist and hip lines. Extend to required hem length and square hemline to CF line.

Note: The example is to hip length and the numbers for widths are in brackets.

2.
Temporarily close the side bust dart. Mark points 1.5cm beyond waist and 1cm beyond hemline. Draw a new side seam curving gently inwards below the underarm and straightening out through the new waist and hem point. Draw a slash line from hem to BP. Cut out pattern following the new side seam.

3.
Cut up slash line from hem to BP and close the bust dart so that the hem opens out. Measure the width of this opening and note, as the back will open the same (10cm).

4.
Draw an extra slash line from hem to underarm. Cut up this new line and spread adding extra width at the hem (4cm).

5.
Retrace the whole pattern drawing a good curve at the hemline, adjusting where the hem has changed.

6.
Grain line: if cutting the garment without a CF seam, the grain will be through CF. If cutting the garment with a CF seam, mark the grain line through the centre of the pattern, this spreads the flare more equally.

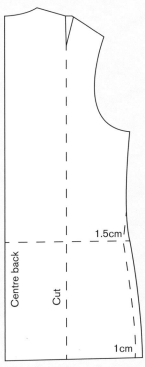

Prep pattern back

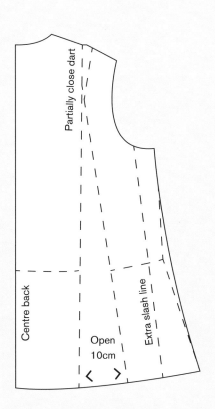

Intermediate pattern back

Step-by-step

BACK

1.
Prepare by tracing around the back bodice block, marking all relevant darts, waist and hip lines. Extend to required hem length and square hemline to CF line.

2.
Mark points 1.5cm beyond the waist, and 1cm beyond the hemline. Draw a new side seam curving gently inwards below the underarm and straightening out through the new waist and hem point. Draw a slash line from hemline to end of shoulder dart. Cut out pattern following new side seam.

3.
Cut up slash line from hem to end of dart, close dart enough to add the same extra width as the front (10cm). Draw an extra slash line from hem to underarm. Cut up this line and spread extra width at the hem (4cm).

Note: There will still be some dart left.

4.
Retrace the whole pattern, drawing a good curve at the hem, and adjusting where the hem has changed.

5.
Grain line: As for front.

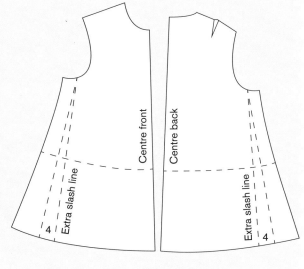

Final pattern front   Final pattern back

Shape in design   **Hourglass**
Linear   Dome
Inverted triangle   Lantern
Square   Cocoon
Trapeze   Balloon

HOURGLASS

3

The hourglass is one of the most popular shapes as it echoes the female body, and can vary from figure-hugging to quite voluminous and extreme emphasis on the hips. It is an easy shape to achieve because it relies on the body shape to make it work and can be fitted on a tailor's dummy successfully. Emphasis of shoulders and hips can create an illusion of a smaller waist, so these relative proportions are considered when designing.

A well-controlled, fitted shape such as the hourglass benefits from panel lines. Panel lines incorporate the darts into seams so that there are no points, such as BP, and can be curved for a good fit. Chapter 2 explains panel lines in more detail (see pages 44–49).

The example given also introduces a curved line from the armhole crossing over the BP to CF line, and transferring the bust dart into the curved line. This separates the upper bodice section and is called a yoke. The back shows a straight yoke section at the top and incorporates the shoulder dart.

Caroline Herrera
We designers always have fantasies in our heads, but the difficult task is to make them reality.

Shape in design	**Hourglass**
Linear	Dome
Inverted triangle	Lantern
Square	Cocoon
Trapeze	Balloon

CREATING A CLASSIC HOURGLASS DRESS WITH FRONT AND BACK YOKES

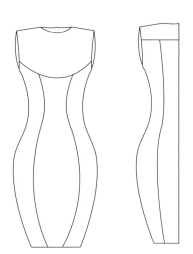

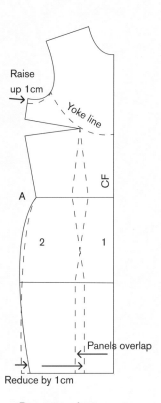

Prep pattern front

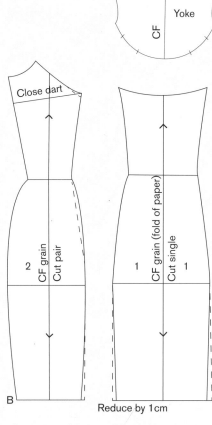

Front yoke, side front panel and centre front panel

Step-by-step

FRONT

1.
Trace off front basic bodice with bust dart in side seam and extend to hem length. Raise UP (underarm point) 1cm for a sleeveless dress.

2.
Draw new side seam from waist extending outwards to accentuate hips and reduce 1cm at hem (B). A pattern master may help to achieve a good line.

3.
Draw a curved yoke line from armhole through BP square to CF. Mark balance points before separating.

4.
Draw panel lines to include waist darts, adding extra width at the hip. The panel lines will cross over each other. Add balance points along the seams.

CREATING PANELS

5.
Separate yoke. Create a whole pattern piece by placing CF on fold of paper.

6.
Trace off separate panel sections, copy side seam shape A–B so that the hips extend and hem reduces by 1cm. Fold bust dart away – it will move into the yoke seam.

Create a whole pattern for centre panel as yoke.

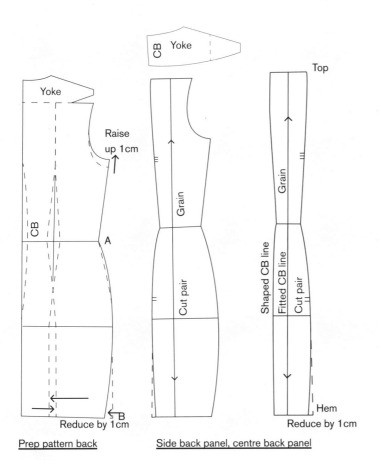

Prep pattern back

Side back panel, centre back panel

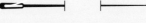

TROUBLESHOOTING

Lay front panel lines together, just below the yoke, as they would be seamed, then place yoke to meet CF and panel lines. The top of the panel lines will need to be redrawn as they will be uneven in length, so use a tracing wheel to transfer the correct lines. (Note: Corrections are redrawn as solid lines in pattern diagrams, dotted lines are original lines.)

TROUBLESHOOTING

Check all panel patterns for symmetry of shape and length by overlaying each panel; for example, turn over side front to lay on centre front – it should be possible to see the lines through the pattern paper. Check all in sequence and correct as necessary.

BACK

1.
Trace off back bodice and extend to hem length as front. Raise UP (underarm point) 1cm for a sleeveless dress.

2.
Draw new side seam from waist extending outwards to accentuate hips and reduce 1cm at hem (B). A pattern master may help to achieve a good line.

3.
Draw yoke line square to CB through shoulder dart point to armhole. Mark balance points before separating.

4.
Draw panel lines to include waist darts, adding extra width at the hip. The panel lines will cross over each other. Add balance points along the seams.

5.
Reduce waist at CB by 1cm and reshape CB line.

CREATING PANELS

6.
Cut and separate yoke. Close shoulder dart away and smooth line, taking away the point of the dart.

7.
Trace off separate panel sections, copy side seam shape A–B so that the hips extend and hem reduces by 1cm.

[Case study]
Kashaf Khalique

An architectural expression of the hourglass shape has full hips supported by a padded under roll shaped to the waist line. Large diagonal darts take the extra hip width away and were modelled on the dummy using a padded support. The 'origami' shapes in the front take advantage of the bust dart position and hide them away.

This design by Kashaf Khalique has been inspired by Dior's hourglass shape, and origami.

Final garment
The hourglass shape has exaggerated hips, created by deep, slanted waist darts. The shape is supported by a hip roll.

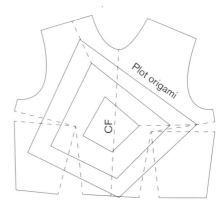

Full front
The origami shapes are plotted with aligning corners radiating from the centre.

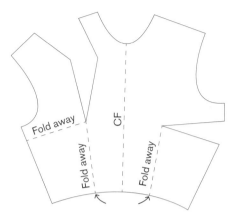

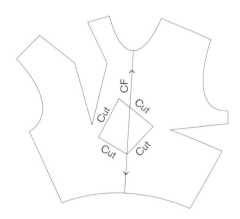

Adding darts
A new dart from shoulder to BP is drawn, aligning with a top corner of the origami. The bust and waist darts are moved to here. On the other side, the side dart to BP is cut and the waist dart is folded away.

Attaching the origami
The central seams of the origami insertions are traced through. This area will need to be cut for seaming.

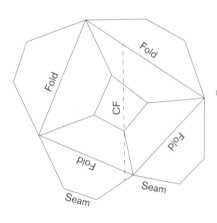

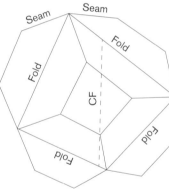

Origami shapes
The extensions fold back and are cut and seamed to create the underside of the origami shape.

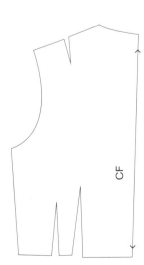

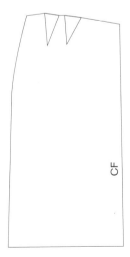

Back bodice
The bodice has two waist darts to match the skirt darts.

Back skirt
This has deep slanted waist darts to create full hips.

Front skirt
Also with deep slanted waist darts.

Shape in design   Hourglass
Linear   **Dome**
Inverted triangle   Lantern
Square   Cocoon
Trapeze   Balloon

DOME

3

This architectural shape rounds the shoulders and encloses the arms in a strong silhouette. The shape is best achieved using fabrics which will hold the shape, so soft drape fabrics are not likely to work. The arms are restricted by the angle of the sleeve, so reasonable width around the sleeve hem is desirable. This is achieved by increasing the width in pattern diagrams.

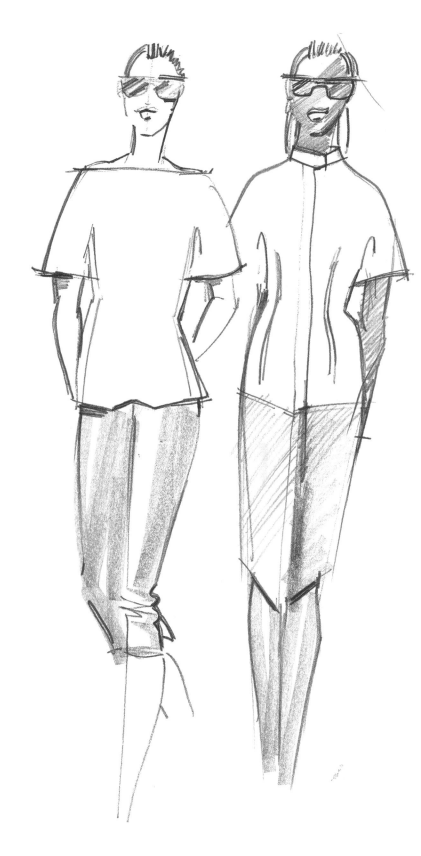

View magazine

Future modern curves and organically softened shapes provide inspiration in architecture and fashion.

	Shape in design	Hourglass
	Linear	**Dome**
	Inverted triangle	Lantern
	Square	Cocoon
	Trapeze	Balloon

3

CREATING THE DOME SHAPE

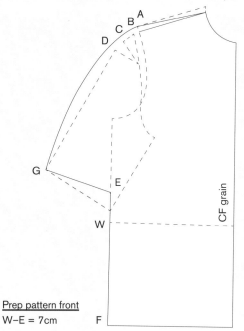

NP (1cm lower)

Prep pattern front
W–E = 7cm

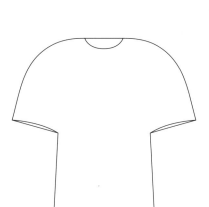

Step-by-step

FRONT

1.
Trace off front bodice with dart in armhole position to hem length (hip). Draw a new shoulder line 1cm lower – this moves the line forward to the front.

2.
Trace off sleeve block, draw a line 4cm down the centre line and square out to either side. Cut out sleeve and separate along centre line. Slash across construction line.

3.
Place the sleeve crown 1cm away from the SP. Open slash line approx 2cm so that the elbow line drops and touches the side seam of the body (see dotted lines).

4.
Raise SP 1cm (to the original SP). Mark point E 7cm above the waist for sleeve hem. Draw in a new shoulder and top sleeve line curving from NP position upwards through the SP, maintaining a good rounded curve and continuing down slightly wider than the original sleeve.

5.
Draw sleeve hemline square to the new top sleeve curve to meet point E.

6.
Complete pattern by connecting E–F in a straight line and squaring a hem across to CF.

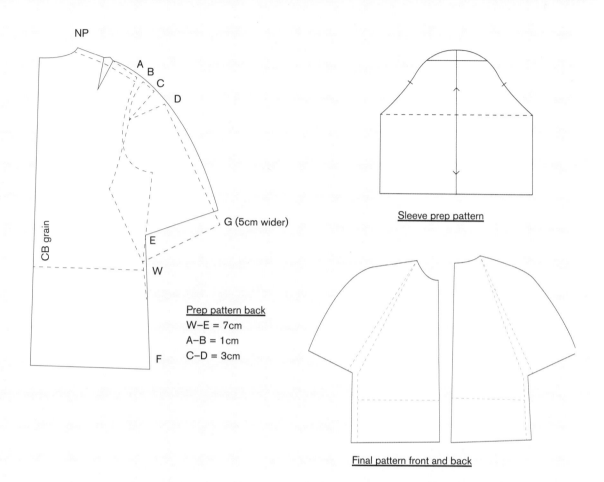

NP

CB grain

A
B
C
D

G (5cm wider)

E

W

F

Prep pattern back
W–E = 7cm
A–B = 1cm
C–D = 3cm

Sleeve prep pattern

Final pattern front and back

Step-by-step

BACK

1.
Trace off back bodice to hem length (hip). Move shoulder line forward 1cm.

2.
Trace off sleeve block, draw a line 4cm down the centre line and square out to either side. Cut out sleeve and separate along centre line. Slash across construction line.

3.
Place the sleeve crown 1cm away from the SP. Open slash line approx 2cm so that the elbow line drops and touches the side seam of the body (see dotted lines).

4.
Raise SP 1cm. Mark point E 7cm above the waist for sleeve hem. Draw in a new shoulder and top sleeve line curving from the dart position upwards through the new SP, maintaining a good rounded curve and continuing down slightly wider than the original sleeve.

5.
Draw sleeve hemline square to the new top sleeve curve to meet point E.

6.
Complete pattern by connecting E–F in a straight line and squaring a hem across to CB.

TROUBLESHOOTING

To create more movement add extra width by slashing a line from the point at which the sleeve meets the side seam up to the NP. Add width (3cm) and redraw the side seam and sleeve hem. Do this back and front.

Inspired by artist Garry Fabian Miller, who creates 'camera-less' photographs, this collection is all about circles of blending light and colour appearing from a black surface. Strong silhouettes and construction are important elements in Anna's work; in this collection simple, bold round shapes were constructed, often involving just one pattern piece shaped by darts and folds. All prints are individually engineered in each garment, following the line of the garment. Blending colours and light are framed by darkness, using light-reflecting materials such as grosgrain, patent leather and nylon mesh. Hidden elements of luxury in the form of fine crystal fabric appear throughout the collection; for example, in the sides of sleeves and hems, and in the boxy cut-outs of the wedges of the custom-made shoes.

'Illume' collection final garments

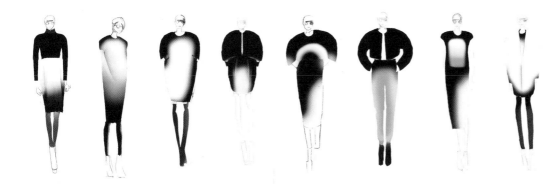

'Illume' collection final line-up

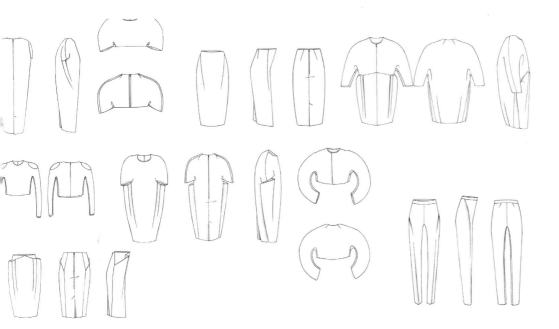

Sketchbook developments

Shape in design   Hourglass
Linear   Dome
Inverted triangle   **Lantern**
Square   Cocoon
Trapeze   Balloon

LANTERN

3

The lantern shape is created by introducing a horizontal seam at the level where the fullness is needed. The position can vary depending on the design, and is the same process for a sleeve pattern. The lantern seam length is increased through the slash and spread method. The fabric will determine the result: a stiff fabric will stand out and a heavy or soft fabric will fall. A more adventurous lantern seam line can be wavy or asymmetrical.

View magazine

Curve-3D contour lines create modern organic shapes... with roundness showing over the curve of the hip or in a gently rounded lantern skirt.

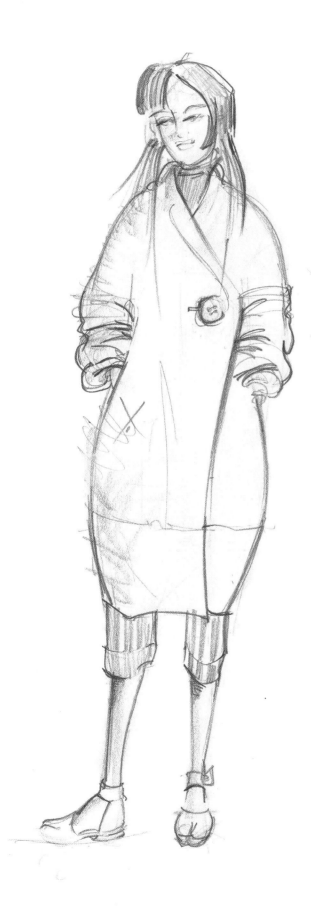

Shape in design	Hourglass
Linear	Dome
Inverted triangle	**Lantern**
Square	Cocoon
Trapeze	Balloon

3

CREATING THE LANTERN SHAPE

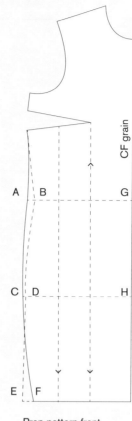

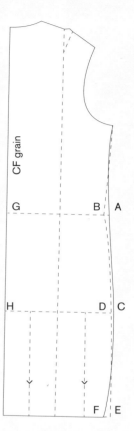

Prep pattern front   Prep pattern back

CURVES

The joining of the two curves, which are convex and concave, create the lantern effect.

Step-by-step

FRONT

1.
Trace off the front bodice block and move the bust dart into the side seam. Mark all relevant information. Extend to the length required (46cm from waist).

2.
Side seam: Mark points 1.5cm (A–B) beyond waistline, 1cm (C–D) beyond hip line and 2cm (E–F) inwards at hemline. Close bust dart and draw side seam gently curving inward from UP and outward through A to C and inward to F. Reopen bust dart.

3.
Lantern line: Square a seam line to CF for lantern line G–H (24cm). Draw a slash line squared from the hem to the BP. Draw two more slash lines only to the lantern seam line and equally either side of the first slash line. Mark balance points before cutting out shape and separating along this line.

ADDING FLARE TO SEPARATED PIECES

4.
Upper front: Slash upward from seam line to BP. Close the bust dart completely to open the hem (10cm). More flare can be added using the slash and spread method if required. Draw a good curved seam and measure.

5.
Lower front: Slash down all three lines from the lantern seam line to hemline. Open each section equally so that it measures the same as the upper seam line length (3.3cm, 3.3cm and 3.4cm). Draw a good curved seam and check it is the same length as the upper front seam.

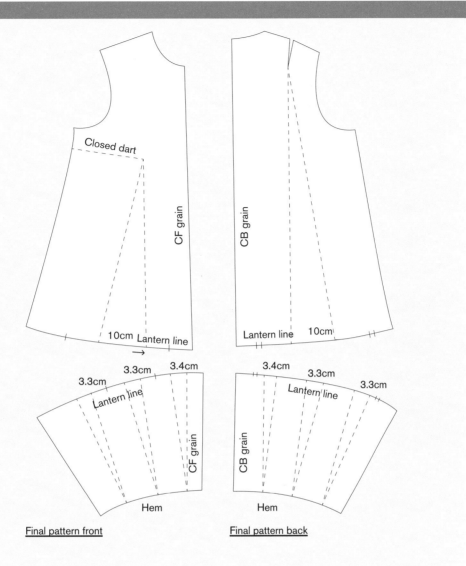

Final pattern front

Final pattern back

Step-by-step

BACK

1.
Trace off the back bodice
block, extending to the
length required
(46cm). Mark all relevant
information.

2.
Side seam: Mark points
1.5cm (A–B) beyond
waistline, 1cm (C–D) beyond
hip line and 2cm (E–F)
inwards at hemline. Close
bust dart and draw side
seam gently curving inward
from UP and outward
through A to C and inward
to F. Reopen bust dart.

3.
Lantern line: Square a seam
line to CB for lantern line
G–H (24cm). Draw a slash
line squared from the hem
to the end of shoulder dart.
Draw two more slash lines
only to the lantern seam
line and equally either
side of the first slash line.
Mark balance points before
cutting out shape and
separating along this line.
Use different balance marks
to front so it is easier to
identify pieces.

4.
Upper back: Slash upward
from seam line to shoulder
dart. Close the dart enough
just to open the hem the
same as the front (10cm).
More flare can be added
using the slash and spread
method if required. Draw
a good curved seam and
measure.

5.
Lower back: Slash down all
three lines from the seam
line to hemline. Open each
section equally so that it
measures the same as the
upper seam line length
(3.3cm, 3.3cm and 3.4cm).
Draw a good curved seam
and check it is the same
length as the upper
back seam.

Shape in design   Hourglass
Linear   Dome
Inverted triangle   Lantern
Square   **Cocoon**
Trapeze   Balloon

COCOON

3

A cocoon shape does what it says: it cocoons the body. It will be necessary to reduce the volume of fabric at the hem (and/or the top) using darts or pleats and folds.

The pattern example shown on the following pages is drafted from a kimono sleeve and uses darts at the hem to reduce and distribute volume in the body, drawing the shape in towards the hem. This creates a rounded shoulder line and side seam, cocooning the body. The darts can be replaced by stitched tucks or folds, or turned into dart seams. Increased volume can be added in pleated folds for a soft, full cocoon. The fabric used will determine the outcome of the cocoon: a stiff solid fabric will make it stand out in a strong silhouette, and a softer, lighter-weight fabric will drop into a flatter cocoon silhouette.

View magazine
Sleek architectural forms: sculptural curves, cocoons, fluid moving sweeping lines. It's anti-angular, modernist and pure.

Shape in design	Hourglass
Linear	Dome
Inverted triangle	Lantern
Square	**Cocoon**
Trapeze	Balloon

3

CREATING THE COCOON SHAPE

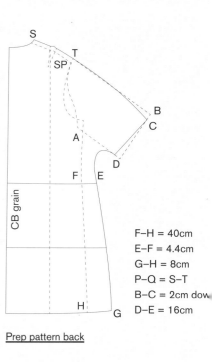
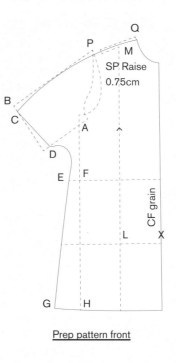

F–H = 40cm
E–F = 4.4cm
G–H = 8cm
P–Q = S–T
B–C = 2cm dow
D–E = 16cm

Prep pattern front   Prep pattern back

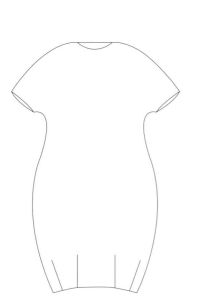

Step-by-step

BACK

1.
Trace off back bodice block extending to hem length (40cm from waist). Trace off sleeve block, move centre line 1cm to front and separate along this line. Move shoulder line 1cm forward.

Follow instructions for kimono block (see page 120).

2.
Pitch sleeve from the forward SP to the underarm 2cm down and in along the side seam through point A. Draw sleeve to elbow length (see dotted lines in diagram).

3.
B–C = 2cm. Draw in a new extended shoulder line, raising SP enough to create a gently rounded line to C. Square across to D.

4.
Widen through waist and hem.
E–F= 4.4cm
G–H = 8cm
Curve a line D–E (16cm), then straighten to G. Square side seam and curve to CB. Measure side seam length as it must match the front.

CREATING THE COCOON

5.
Cut out the pattern.
L–X = 14cm. L–M squared line through waist to end of shoulder dart. Close shoulder dart to open hem. L–O = 12cm.

6.
Extend hemline to allow for cocoon effect at hem X–Z = 8cm. Along this new line plot equally spaced darts to remove excess volume at the hemline. In the example, the darts are 8cm deep and spaced roughly 8cm apart. You will have half CB dart and half side seam dart, and two full darts on your pattern, balancing the distribution of volume around the body.

7.
Draw the length of the darts as long as you want them (15cm), keeping the midline square to the hemline. The darts can be cut away to become seamed darts or partially stitched and released in shaped pleats.

8.
Mark points 1.5cm out at the hip and 4cm in at the hemline. Complete the shape by drawing a curved side seam from the waist, passing through extended hip point (1.5cm) and curving to meet the dart end point (4cm) inside the side seam.

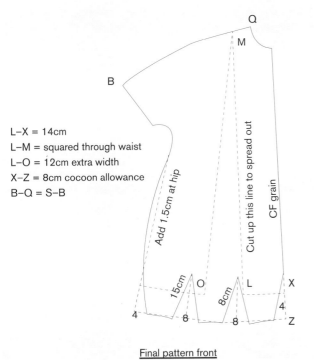

L–X = 14cm
L–M = squared through waist
L–O = 12cm extra width
X–Z = 8cm cocoon allowance
B–Q = S–B

Add 1.5cm at hip

15cm
8cm

Cut up this line to spread out

CF grain

Q
M
B
O
L
X
4
8
8
Z

Final pattern front

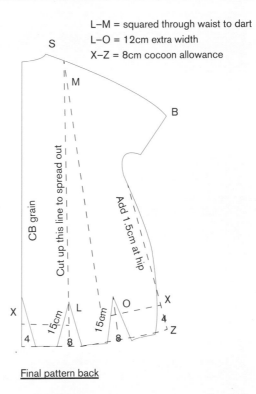

L–M = squared through waist to dart
L–O = 12cm extra width
X–Z = 8cm cocoon allowance

CB grain

Cut up this line to spread out

Add 1.5cm at hip

S
M
B
X
15cm
L
15cm
O
X
4
8
8
Z

Final pattern back

Step-by-step

FRONT

1.

Trace off front bodice block extending to hem length (40cm from waist). Extend shoulder line the width of back shoulder dart so F and B lengths are the same. Raise SP 0.75cm.
Trace off sleeve block, move centre line 1cm to front and separate along this line. Move shoulder line 1cm forward.

Follow instructions for kimono block.

2.

Pitch sleeve from the forward SP to the underarm, 2cm down and in along the side seam through point A. Draw sleeve to elbow length (see dotted lines in diagram).

3.

B–C = 2cm. Draw in a new extended shoulder line, raising SP enough to create a gently rounded line to C. Square across to D.

4.

Widen through waist and hem.
E–F= 4.4cm
G–H= 8cm
Curve a line D–E (16cm), then straighten to G. Square side seam and curve to CB. Measure side seam length as it must match the front.

Note: Measure the length of the curve from waist to sleeve hemline, it must be the same as the back (16cm). Adjust as necessary. The curves will not be the same shape as the angles if the front and back are not the same. If you have difficulty in drawing successful matching curves, adjust the shape either front or back to make it easier.

CREATING THE COCOON

5.

Cut out the pattern.
L–X = 14cm. L–M = squared line through waist. Slash up this line from L and spread adding hem width. L–O = 12cm.

6.

Extend hemline to allow for cocoon effect at hem X–Z = 8cm. Along this new line plot equally spaced darts to remove excess volume at the hemline. In the example, the darts are 8cm deep and spaced roughly 8cm apart. You will have half CB dart and half side seam dart, and two full darts on your pattern, balancing the distribution of volume around the body.

7.

Draw the length of the darts as long as you want them (15cm), keeping the midline square to the hemline. The darts can be cut away to become seamed darts or partially stitched and released in shaped pleats.

8.

Mark points 1.5cm out at the hip and 4cm in at the hemline. Complete the shape by drawing a curved side seam from the waist passing through extended hip point (1.5cm) and curving to meet the dart end point (4cm) inside the side seam.

Note: You can use the side seam shape from the back and trace through to guarantee the lines being the same. To do this use a light box or lay your pattern one on top of the other and trace through with a tracing wheel.

102 **Shape**

Shape in design	Hourglass
Linear	Dome
Inverted triangle	Lantern
Square	Cocoon
Trapeze	**Balloon**

BALLOON

3

The balloon shape was popular in the 1980s and has been revived several times since, whenever there is a trend for volume. A balloon can be introduced in many places on the body and may not be the complete overall silhouette; it may be in the lower section of a sleeve, for example. Generally, the ballooning fabric in a skirt will need to be controlled by an under fabric/lining. This helps to draw the fabric under to create a voluminous balloon. A balloon top will have gathers held by some kind of finish such as elastic, drawstring, cuff or binding, so will not need an under fabric/lining.

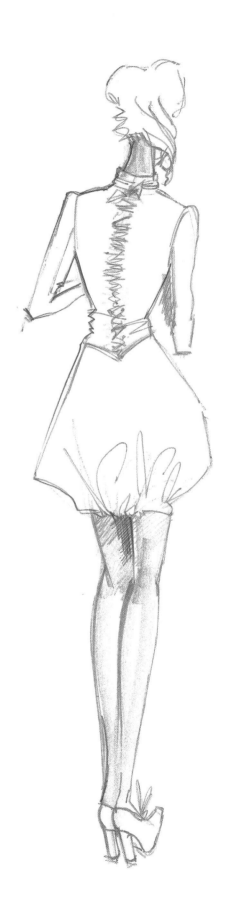

Frida Giannini
Fashion today is a balancing act between high and low tech.

Shape in design   Hourglass
Linear   Dome
Inverted triangle   Lantern
Square   Cocoon
Trapeze   **Balloon**

3

BALLOON SKIRT

Volume in this skirt is created using a circle, an easy method of introducing a lot of volume at the hem with only two seams. The waistline remains the same size and the hem is full and gathered (or pleated depending on the look you want to create). It is important to consider the fabric for the desired effect: a stiff fabric will stick out more than a soft or heavy fabric.

Radius = circumference divided by 6.28.

ESTABLISHING THE WAISTLINE

To draw the waistline circle (circumference), the radius has to be established. This is calculated by dividing the circumference by 6.28. For example, a waist of 68cm is 68/6.28 = 10.8cm radius. Use the radius to draw the waistline circle.

ADDING GATHERS

If there are to be gathers at the waist, calculate how much is needed by a fabric gather test. It is common to double the amount for gathers, so if this was the case the circumference would be 136cm and the radius 21.6cm.

CREATING THE BALLOON SHAPE

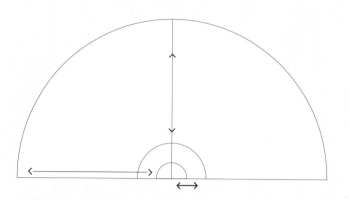

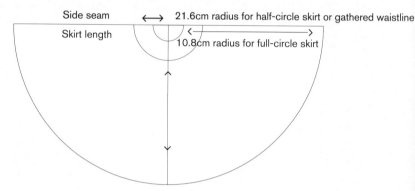

Side seam   21.6cm radius for half-circle skirt or gathered waistline
Skirt length   10.8cm radius for full-circle skirt

Pair of half-circle patterns

Step-by-step

TOP SKIRT

1.
Front and back: Use the radius (10.8cm) to draw the waistline measurement circle.

Important: Draw the side seam allowance first along the edge of the paper and start the radius from the seam line.

2.
Measure the length of the skirt equally from the waistline circle, allowing extra length (6cm) for turning the fabric back into the lining.

3.
Draw a smooth curve for the hemline circle, joining the measured points of the skirt length.

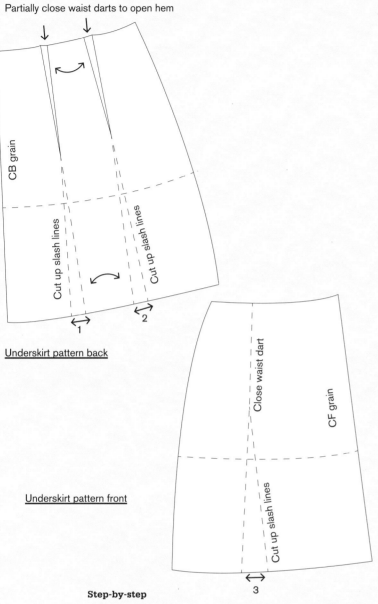

Partially close waist darts to open hem

CB grain

Cut up slash lines

Cut up slash lines

1

2

Underskirt pattern back

Close waist dart

CF grain

Cut up slash lines

Underskirt pattern front

3

LINING (UNDERSKIRT)

To create the 'balloon' effect there must be a lining cut shorter than the actual hem to which the gathered outer hem is sewn, so that it draws the hem fabric up forming folds on the actual hemline. Therefore, you need to calculate the amount of 'balloon' you want in the garment, and the difference between the top layer of the skirt and the lining. The top layer will be longer than the lining but cannot be excessively longer as it will fall with gravity and lose the balloon effect.

FABRIC WIDTH

It is likely you will make the pattern and garment in two halves rather than one complete circle due to paper and fabric width, but the radius stays the same.

Step-by-step

LINING (UNDERSKIRT)

1.
Trace off the front and back basic skirt blocks, marking in all relevant information. The length of the lining will be shorter by half the hem extension at the top skirt, for example if the top skirt is extended by 6cm then the lining is shortened by 3cm. This may need to be adjusted at the fitting stage.

2.
Draw slash lines squared from the hem to the dart ends in front and back.

3.
Front: Cut up the slash line to the dart end, open enough to allow for the waist dart to close away completely. This will widen the hem.

Note: If you want less hem width, only open as far as you want, but the dart will still exist at the waist.

4.
Back: Cut up slash lines, close darts equally to allow the two slashed sections together to be the same width as the front extra width to balance front and back. Usually there will be some dart left at the back waist.

5.
Check the hem width allows for the top to be gathered enough for fullness, if not reduce.

Shape in design
Linear
Inverted triangle
Square
Trapeze

Hourglass
Dome
Lantern
Cocoon
Balloon

BALLOON TOP

3

This example is based on the kimono block and uses the slash and spread method to create volume in the basic pattern shape. To create the balloon effect there are small gathers at the neck with more at the wrist and hem, and an elbow-length kimono/batwing sleeve.

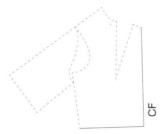

Basic prep kimono block

BATWING

This preparation stage pattern can also be used for a basic batwing sleeve pattern block.

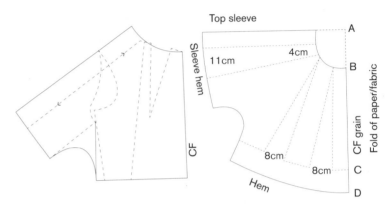

Intermediate pattern front

Final pattern front
A–B = 7cm
C–D = 8cm

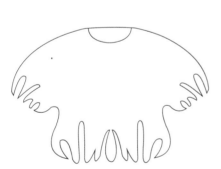

Step-by-step

BALLOON TOP

Preparation
Prepare front and back by creating a basic shape following instructions for the kimono block.

Note: The bust dart is moved to the neck so that it creates a few gathers.

FRONT

1.
Draft the 'kimono shape' for the underarm seam and sleeve length (40cm). Draw at least two slash lines from neck to hem but not parallel to CF so that they slope outward from the neck. Add at least one slash line from wrist to neck, following the top sleeve slope. Cut out shape.

2.
On a new piece of paper draw two construction lines square to each other for the CF and sleeve top line. This must be longer to allow for adding length and width to the new pattern (approx 58cm both ways).

3.
Creating volume: Place the CF line of the pattern against a line with neckline approx 7cm down from the top (A–B). Cut up slash lines from hem to neck only on body section and separate line nearest sleeve top.

4.
Spread body sections 8cm at hem, sleeve section opens 4cm at neck and 11cm at sleeve hem. The sleeve top line should reach the squared line so that the whole pattern opens out as a quarter circle.

5.
Add extra length at the hemline (C–D = 8cm) for balloon effect when gathered in and draw smooth curved lines for neck and hems. All these lines will be gathered to fit.

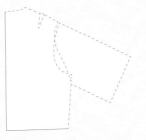

Basic prep kimono block

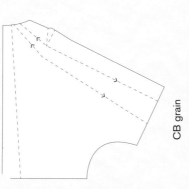

Intermediate pattern back

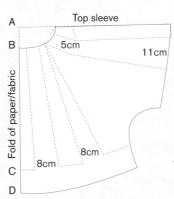

Final pattern back
A–B = 7cm
C–D = 8cm

BACK

6.
Draft the 'batwing shape' for the underarm seam and sleeve length (40cm). Make sure the side seam lengths match front and back.

Draw at least two slash lines from neck to hem but not parallel to CB so that they slope outward from the neck. Add at least one slash line from wrist to neck, following the top sleeve slope. Cut out shape, close shoulder dart away – this will bend the sleeve slope.

7.
On a new piece of paper draw two construction lines square to each other for the CB and sleeve top line. This must be longer to allow for adding length and width to the new pattern (approx 58cm both ways).

8.
Creating volume: Place the CB line of the pattern against a line with neckline approx 7cm down from the top (A–B). Cut up slash lines from hem to neck only on body section and separate line nearest sleeve top.

9.
Spread body sections 8cm at hem, sleeve section opens 5cm at neck and 11cm at sleeve hem. The sleeve top line should reach the squared line so that the whole pattern opens out as a quarter circle. Ignore sleeve bend due to closed dart, keep to straight line.

10.
Add extra length (C–D = 8cm) at the hemline for balloon effect when gathered in and draw smooth curved lines for neck and hems. All these lines will be gathered to fit.

4

SLEEVES, COLLARS AND CIRCLES

A design is defined by a number of elements: overall silhouette, shape, fit, balance and relative proportions of shoulders, collars and cuffs, details such as pockets, and colour and textural values of the cloth. It is precisely these elements – the ratio of shoulder- to hip-width, the size and shape of an armhole, the positioning of a pocket – that reflect changes in fashion. This chapter explores the fundamentals of sleeves, collars and circles, offering examples that can lead to more complex cutting.

110 Sleeve fundamentals

112 Set-in sleeves

118 Grown-on sleeves

126 Sleeve cuffs

128 Collar fundamentals

130 One-piece collars

134 Two-piece collars

136 Circles and ruffles

4

Sleeve fundamentals
Set-in sleeves
Grown-on sleeves
Sleeve cuffs

Collar fundamentals
One-piece collars
Two-piece collars
Circles and ruffles

SLEEVE FUNDAMENTALS

With a unique sleeve design, and no other design features, a garment can look extraordinary. Sleeves are an important part of pattern cutting; the pattern cutter must be sensitive to this – after all, the exact length and angle of a shoulder line could be critical to the designer's 'handwriting' of the season. A pattern cutter must also consider the best type, shape and fit of sleeve to express the design. There is a distinct relationship between shoulder and sleeve, and this must be taken into account when drafting patterns.

Sleeves can be traced through their history by their relationship to the bodice and the resulting silhouettes that these combinations produced. For example, the eighteenth-century short puffed sleeve slipping away from the shoulder, or the nineteenth-century Victorian 'leg-of-mutton' sleeve often moving into the shoulder. Sleeves can express social and cultural behaviour and change, and even follow their own trends. The raised padded shoulder of the 1940s, for example, expressed the masculine role of women during the war, and the 1980s extended shoulder expressed the male-dominated corporate world, into which women were entering.

This chapter shows some examples of sleeves which can be adapted according to the design. Techniques for adding flare or volume, introducing seams for fit or shape can be used to alter the sleeve, and are exampled in other chapters of the book.

Vivienne Westwood

Fashion is very important. It is life enhancing and, like everything that gives you pleasure, it is worth doing well.

Left
<u>Alexander McQueen SS10</u>
An interesting sleeve can turn
even the simplest garment
into a striking design.

112   **Sleeves, Collars and Circles**

Sleeve fundamentals
Set-in sleeves
Grown-on sleeves
Sleeve cuffs

Collar fundamentals
One-piece collars
Two-piece collars
Circles and ruffles

SET-IN SLEEVES

4

A sleeve block is drafted according to the size and depth of the armhole, so the depth of the crown will vary according to changes made to the bodice block (fitting the bodice tighter or raising the armhole, for example). The block created from Winifred Aldrich's instructions has 'ease' on the crown for an easy fit over the top arm. Reducing the sleeve width results in a tighter fit on the top arm, but raising the underarm of the body can help as it allows the arm to move without dragging the body with it. The examples over the next few pages show basic variations of the set-in sleeve.

SEMI-FITTED SLEEVE

A loose sleeve allows the elbow to move. If the sleeve is reduced in width, it compromises movement. The sleeve needs to be shaped to the arm, and this is done by creating a dart at the elbow.

SEMI-FITTED SLEEVE

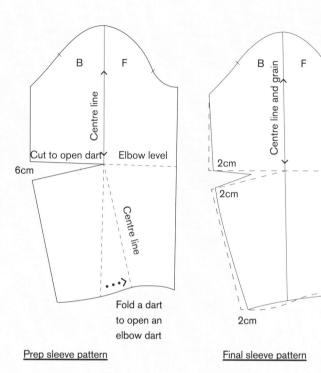

Prep sleeve pattern

Final sleeve pattern

Step-by-step

1.
Trace the basic sleeve block, marking in all relevant lines and balance points. Cut out.

2.
From the back, cut along the elbow line to the centre line. Fold a dart away below the elbow to the wrist to open a 6cm dart at elbow level.

3.
On the front, mark points 2cm in at elbow level and 2cm in at wrist. Draw a curved line from the underarm point through these points for a more fitted seam.

4.
On the back, mark points 2cm in at elbow on both sides of the elbow dart and 2cm at wrist. Draw a curved line from the underarm point through these points as on the front.

5.
Draw a shorter dart position within the dart opening (approximately halfway to centre line).

6.
Complete the sleeve by connecting the new wrist points with a curved line, meeting the seams at short right angles.

FITTED SLEEVE

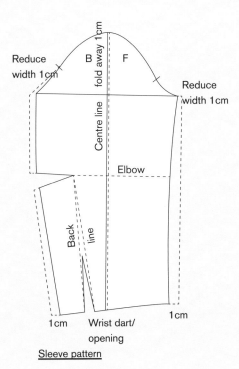

Reduce
width 1cm

B   F

fold away 1cm

Centre line

Reduce
width 1cm

Elbow

Back line

1cm   1cm

Wrist dart/
opening

Sleeve pattern

FITTED SLEEVE

This sleeve example requires the bodice to be reduced in width at the side seams by 1cm each side, and match this reduction in the sleeve width. The sleeve head is also reduced so there is less or no ease in the crown. It also introduces a wrist dart to tighten the wrist – the dart can be used as an opening.

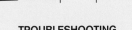

TROUBLESHOOTING

If you want, the sleeve can be reduced further. This will require the darts to increase as the sleeve shapes more to the arm. Firstly, slash across elbow level to open the elbow into a larger dart and fold away a dart at wrist to reduce the width. Do not overdo this, rather increase the size of the wrist dart/opening.

Step-by-step

1.
Trace the semi-fitted sleeve pattern, marking in all relevant lines and balance points, or follow instructions for constructing the semi-fitted sleeve. Cut out.

2.
Fold away 1cm all the way through the centre line to reduce crown ease (0.5cm each side of centre line).

3.
Reduce the width of the sleeve in the front, 1cm all the way through, following the seam curve of the semi-fitted sleeve.

4.
Reduce the width of the sleeve in the back, 1cm all the way through, following the seam curve of the semi-fitted sleeve.

5.
Reduce the wrist by introducing a dart on the back line, parallel to the curved seam line. Bring to meet the elbow dart end point. Redraw the dart length to approximately 13cm.

6.
Close the elbow dart and make true the underarm seam if necessary. Close the wrist dart and draw a curved line for the wrist from seam to seam.

Sleeve fundamentals
Set-in sleeves
Grown-on sleeves
Sleeve cuffs

Collar fundamentals
One-piece collars
Two-piece collars
Circles and ruffles

4

SHIRT SLEEVE

This sleeve keeps the width of the sleeve and adds length for 'overhang'. Alternatively, it can be shortened for deeper cuffs. The extra width can be gathered or pleated into the cuff. There is an opening on the back line for a placket.

SHIRT SLEEVE

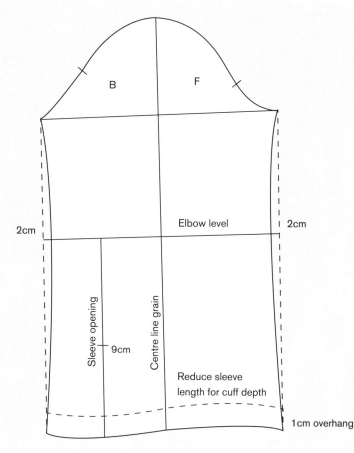

Final pattern

Step-by-step

1.
Trace around the basic sleeve block that matches the bodice you are working with. Mark all relevant lines and balance points.

2.
Mark points inward (2cm) along the elbow line. Connect the underarm and wrist points with a curved line through this point front and back. You can copy one curve to the other side by tracing through with paper folded, aligning the UPs and wrist points.

3.
On the back, square a construction line down from elbow line, midway between the original underarm seam and centre line on the back sleeve. This can also be done by folding the paper and laying the side seam onto the centre line. The crease will be midway.

4.
The sleeve opening is marked on this line up from the wrist (9cm).

5.
If adding pleats to the wrist, plot them according to the width of the cuff. Draw a finished wrist with the pleats folded, and trace through for pleat shaping.

6.
If reducing length for cuff, still allow 'overhang' of at least 1cm.

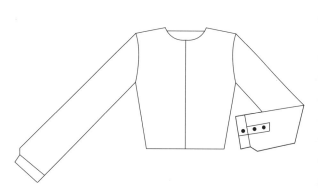

SQUARING THE SHOULDER AND RAISING THE SLEEVE CROWN

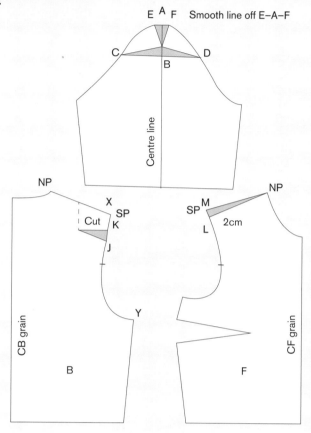

Smooth line off E–A–F

SQUARING THE SHOULDER AND RAISING THE SLEEVE CROWN

A raised or squared shoulder line supported by a shoulder pad creates a squared silhouette but can also prevent garment 'drag' when hanging from the shoulders. It eliminates the back shoulder dart, which interrupts the shoulder line. Before raising the shoulder and sleeve head, the height of the pad should be known, or a pad made to fit the shape and size.

Final pattern

1–2 = 3–4

E–F = 1–2 and 3–4

J–K = L–M

Step-by-step

1.
Back block: Draw a line from the armhole roughly squared to the shoulder dart point. Slash along this line to the dart point and close the shoulder dart away, moving it into the armhole. This will raise the shoulder line at SP. Redraw the armhole from SP to make true the line.

2.
Front block: If the bust dart is in the shoulder then move it to another place. Raise the SP by the measurement of the back armhole dart and draw a new shoulder line from here to NP. If the shoulder pad is smaller or bigger than the raised shoulder then adjust accordingly by raising it or lowering the line at SP.

3.
Sleeve: Trace off the basic sleeve block, marking all relevant lines and balance points. Measure down the centre line from the crown approximately 6cm and square a line across both ways to the edges.

4.
Cut down the centre line and outwards both ways just reaching the edges but not cutting off. Move these pieces upwards in the centre so that the crown opens out. The opening should be the same measurement as the raised shoulder, front and back. Draw in the new sleeve crown. Check the measurements for armhole and sleeve match, with or without ease. A woollen fabric will shrink to fit but a cotton fabric will not need much ease, if any.

116   **Sleeves, Collars   Sleeve fundmentals   Collar fundamentals
and Circles**   **Set-in sleeves**   One-piece collars
Grown-on sleeves   Two-piece collars
Sleeve cuffs   Circles and ruffles

4

SQUARED SHOULDER AND SLEEVE SEAM

This example, with a seam in the sleeve crown, creates a squarer shoulder and the seam gives more control over the shoulder extension. Introducing seams into the sleeve can be used to create a variety of designs, such as strapped sleeves. Squared shoulders were popular in the 1940s, and the 1980s went much further with exaggerated shoulders. A squared shoulder can typically contribute to an inverted triangle shape.

SQUARED SHOULDER AND SLEEVE SEAM

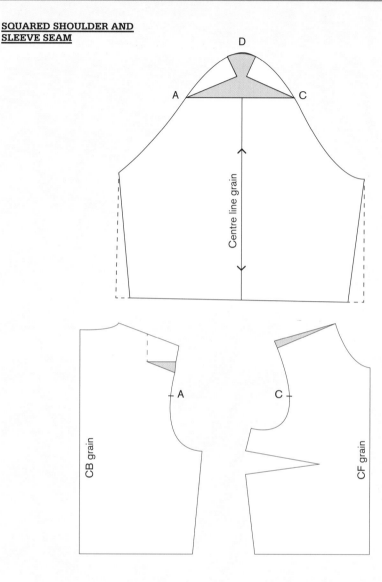

Prep pattern

Step-by-step

1.
Prepare bodice and sleeve as for the squared shoulder and raised crown. Mark points A and C 7cm down from SP on the armholes where the extended shoulder seam will meet – this is best done by placing the pattern on the dummy so you will know exactly where it will be. Transfer these measurements to the sleeve crown A and C.

2.
On the sleeve measure down the centre line the measurement you want to extend the shoulder line (D–B = 6cm). Draw a curved line from A to C through B on the centre line. Mark balance points on this line.

3.
Crown: Trace/copy this top shape off, marking the balance points. Draw equally spaced slash lines along line A–B–C, fanning out from the centre line to the sleeve head line A–D–C.

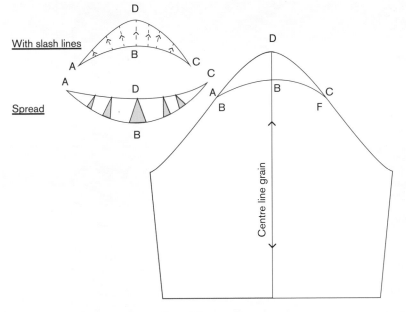

With slash lines

Spread

Centre line grain

Prep sleeve pattern

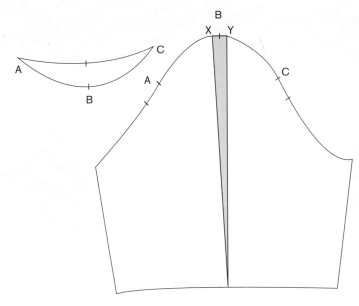

Final sleeve pattern

SEAM LENGTH
The length of the line depends on how much the shoulder will be 'squared', so if the sleeve rises upward from the SP, for example, then the seam line will be longer.

4.
Slash up these lines from A–B–C to the top edge without cutting off. Spread the sections equally both sides, but more in the centre so that the upper and lower seam lines are reversed in shape. Line A–B–C is now a convex curve, and will alter depending on the look.

5.
Sleeve: Slash the remaining sleeve down the centre line to elbow level or hem and spread the crown (X–Y = 2.25cm) so that the top line is the same length as the crown seam A–B–C.

118   **Sleeves, Collars and Circles**

Sleeve fundamentals
Set-in sleeves
Grown-on sleeves
Sleeve cuffs

Collar fundamentals
One-piece collars
Two-piece collars
Circles and ruffles

GROWN-ON SLEEVES

4

Grown-on sleeves describe sleeves where part of the bodice is grown on to the sleeve, or where the sleeve is incorporated entirely into the body.

BASIC RAGLAN SLEEVE

The difference between a raglan sleeve and a set-in sleeve is that part of the bodice is 'grown on' to the sleeve head, taking into account the angle of the shoulder. This will move the sleeve seam diagonally across the body to the neck but keep the underarm as normal. This new line is best drawn whilst the bodice pattern is on the tailor's dummy as it should be a curved line, and you can see immediately if the line looks good and is what is wanted.

The angle of the shoulder stays the same, but the shape can be changed such as raising it for a shoulder pad. The shoulder line is moved forward from the back to the front so that it sits more comfortably.

As there can be a centre sleeve seam on the top line it is also possible to change the shape of the whole sleeve down the centre, from straight to curved. This would add width to the sleeve. It is also possible to remove the underarm seam as there is a top seam. This is done by placing the underarm seams together as one pattern piece.

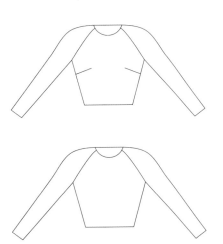

BASIC RAGLAN SLEEVE

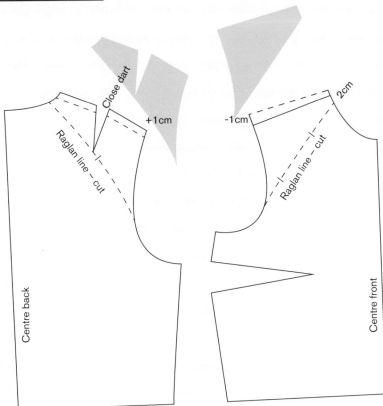

Prep pattern

Step-by-step

FRONT

Pattern example measurements are shown in brackets.

1.
Move the bust dart into the side seam, or anywhere away from the shoulder and neck area.

2.
Move the shoulder line forward by removing 1cm from the block pattern.

3.
Draw a gently curving raglan line from the armhole balance point to the neckline (2cm from new shoulder line). This is best done on a tailor's dummy or person, but not essential. Mark balance points along this line.

4.
Cut away this section from the body for the sleeve. The lower body line can be shaped a little to take away excess fabric, but this can be done at the fit for certainty.

BACK

1.
Move the shoulder line forward by adding 1cm. Make sure the shoulder lengths are still the same.

2.
Draw a gently curved line from the back armhole at a level similar to the front to the neckline, passing on or near the end of the shoulder dart. Mark balance points on this line.

3.
Cut away this section from the body for the sleeve. The lower body line can be shaped a little to take away excess fabric, but this can be done at the fit for certainty.

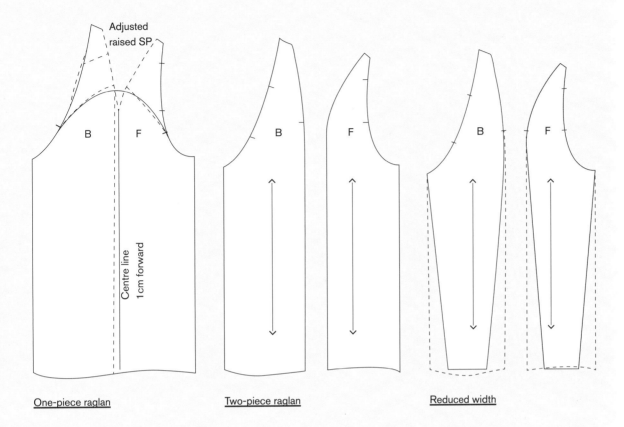

Adjusted raised SP

B F

Centre line 1cm forward

One-piece raglan

B F

Two-piece raglan

B F

Reduced width

CREATING A TWO-PIECE SLEEVE

Trace the one-piece raglan sleeve, transferring all balance points and centre seam line. Cut and separate the front and back. Make true the shoulder shape so that the line is smooth.

REDUCING THE WIDTH OF THE WRIST AND SLEEVE

Reduce the width of the sleeve at the wrist by establishing the size you want then reducing the width by the difference. The underarm line has more reduction than the top line (see diagram). Straighten the bottom of the sleeve at wrist so that the front and back are level.

SLEEVE

1.
Trace around the basic sleeve block, marking the centre line. Move the centre line forward toward the front 1cm and extend the line above the sleeve crown.

2.
Place the front bodice section so that the armhole meets the sleeve at the notch toward the underarm and touches the sleeve crown on the forward centre sleeve line. This often means that the shoulder point is raised above the sleeve head. This is ok as the shape of the lines are not exactly compatible.

3.
Adjust the shoulder dart point to meet the raglan line if it does not already do so, and close the dart.

4.
Place the back bodice section as for the front, making sure the shoulder points are at the same level as the sleeve crown.

5.
Draw around these additions for the new sleeve, making good the line where the back shoulder dart has been closed and the shoulder shape as it meets the sleeve crown. Transfer all balance points.

Sleeve fundamentals
Set-in sleeves
Grown-on sleeves
Sleeve cuffs

Collar fundamentals
One-piece collars
Two-piece collars
Circles and ruffles

4

BASIC KIMONO SLEEVE

In this pattern the sleeve is totally incorporated into the body as one. The angle and depth of the sleeve is determined by the design, but the process would be the same. There are two examples shown which demonstrate the difference in sleeve positioning for different angles. It must be noted that the steeper the angle of the sleeve toward the body, the less movement there will be for the arm. A gusset – a diamond or u-shaped insert – can be added into the body at the tightest point of the underarm curve, which gives extra length and helps movement, but this is limited. There will be a critical point at which it will become impossible to move if the angle is too steep. These sleeves are then cut into sections and become Magyar sleeves, so that the top sleeve stays in one with the body and the lower or under sleeve and body sections become separate. This type of sleeve was popular in the 1950s and 1990s.

BASIC KIMONO SLEEVE

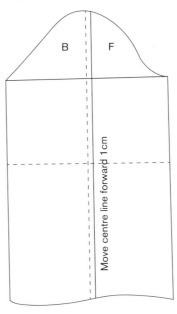

Prep pattern

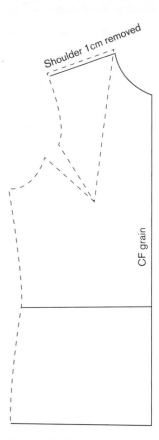

Front bodice block pattern

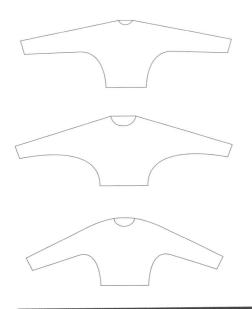

Above
Sleeve slopes
Kimonos have many variations where the shoulder line slopes toward the body.

Step-by-step

Pattern example measurements shown in brackets.

1.
Trace the basic sleeve block, marking in balance points and centre line. Move centre line forward 1cm. Cut out and separate front and back along the new centre line.

2.
Trace the front bodice block and move the dart into the armhole. Move shoulder line forward 1cm by removing 1cm.

3.
Trace the back bodice block and move the shoulder dart into the armhole. Move the shoulder line forward by adding 1cm.

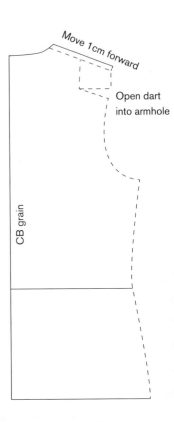

Back bodice block pattern

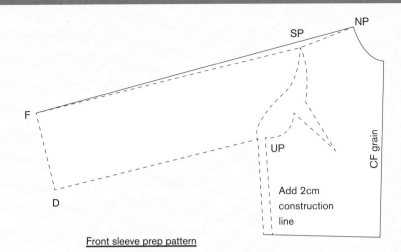

Front sleeve prep pattern

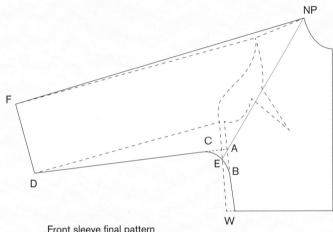

Front sleeve final pattern

W–A = 15cm

A–B = 6cm

A–C = 6cm

A–E = 3cm

FRONT

1.
Draw a construction line 2cm wider and parallel to the side seam.

2.
Place the front sleeve SP and top of crown touching, and UP touching the extended side seam construction line.

3.
From point A (15cm above waist) draw a construction line to sleeve end (D).

4.
Mark points equidistant from this point A–B (6cm) and A–C (6cm). This will guide the curve of the underarm. Draw an extra construction line from NP through point A to E on construction side seam (A–E = 3cm).

5.
Complete the pattern by connecting NP to sleeve end (F) in a straight line and drawing the underarm in a straight line from D, curving from C through E and B, and then straightening to waist on original side seam.

Sleeve fundamentals
Set-in sleeves
Grown-on sleeves
Sleeve cuffs

Collar fundamentals
One-piece collars
Two-piece collars
Circles and ruffles

4

BASIC KIMONO SLEEVE
(continued)

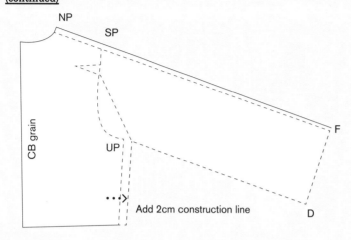

Back sleeve prep pattern

ADJUSTING THE WIDTH OF THE SLEEVE

The width of the wrist can be adjusted by drawing a new underarm line using the same method but with different measurements.

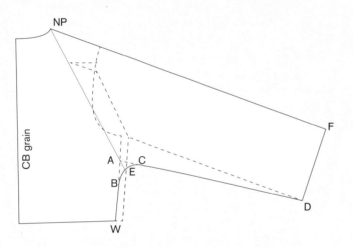

Back sleeve final pattern

BACK

1.
Draw a construction line 2cm wider and parallel to the side seam.

2.
Place the back sleeve SP and top of crown touching and UP touching the extended side seam construction line (NP–F is a straight line).

3.
From point A (15cm above waist), draw a construction line to sleeve end (D).

4.
Mark points equidistant from this point A–B (6cm) and A–C (6cm). This will guide the curve of the underarm. Draw an extra construction line from NP through point A to E on construction side seam (A–E = 3cm).

5.
Complete the pattern by drawing the underarm in a straight line from D, curving from C through E and B, then straightening to waist on original side seam.

STEEPER SLANT FROM SHOULDER

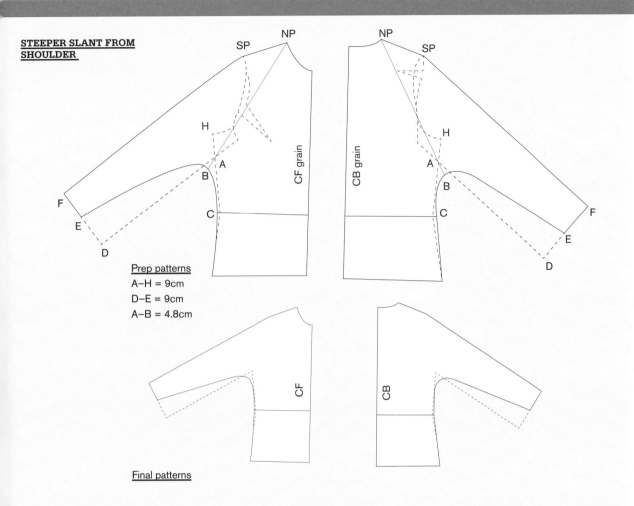

Prep patterns
A–H = 9cm
D–E = 9cm
A–B = 4.8cm

Final patterns

Step-by-step

1.
Prepare the front and back bodice block and sleeve as for the kimono.

2.
Place the front sleeve head touching the SP and swing the sleeve into the body, crossing the side seam 9cm down from H through A (A–H = 9cm). The more the sleeve swings into the body, the more restricted movement becomes. Draw temporary lines marking the sleeve (A–D).

3.
Draw a diagonal construction line from NP through the point where the sleeve crosses the body (A) and extend 5cm beyond A to point B.

4.
Reduce the width at the sleeve end equally from the side seam (D–E = 9cm). Using a French curve, draw the underarm curve from E, curving through B to the waist (C) or hem. The curve is governed by the width of the sleeve. Measure curves E–B and B–C as they must match front and back.

5.
Draw the top shoulder and sleeve line from NP through SP to F, curving and slightly rounding over the shoulder to remove points.

6.
Repeat the process for the back. The underarm lines can be traced through matching C–B and then B–E, and the top line NP–SP to F. Tracing through helps to keep the lines the same length and shape.

7.
Check line lengths and correct if necessary by changing the angle of the lines. Mark balance points along both lines, particularly under the arm where the curves are tight.

124

**Sleeves, Collars
and Circles**

Sleeve fundamentals
Set-in sleeves
Grown-on sleeves
Sleeve cuffs

Collar fundamentals
One-piece collars
Two-piece collars
Circles and ruffles

4

DOLMAN SLEEVE

This sleeve is based on a kimono block, but there is more control in the movement of the underarm because extra length is added to allow the underarm to act like a gusset. Separating the sleeve from the body also offers control of the pitch of the sleeve from the SP by altering the height of the sleeve crown.

DOLMAN SLEEVE

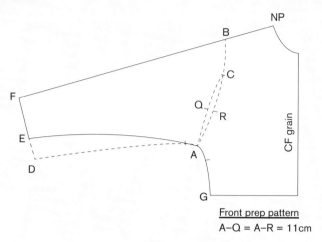

Front prep pattern
A–Q = A–R = 11cm

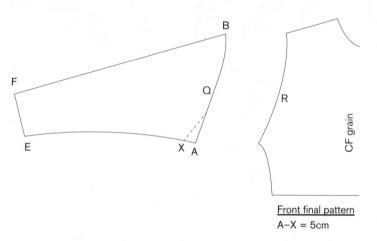

Front final pattern
A–X = 5cm

Step-by-step

Prepare by tracing the basic kimono block front and back.

FRONT

1.
Armhole: Draw a curved armhole line from B (15cm from NP) to side seam (A) according to the design. The depth and shape of the line depends on the design, but you can follow the basic kimono. Square the line as it touches the shoulder line; this prevents a point at sleeve crown.

2.
Start shaping the body armhole from C (15cm from SP). From B draw a curved line to side seam (A–B).

3.
Mark C 11cm down from B on this line. Copy the curve of armhole A–C by folding on a straight construction line A–C and tracing through line A–C from body.

4.
Mark balance points 11cm up from the armhole on body and sleeve armholes (points R and Q).

5.
Reduce the sleeve end (wrist) to the measurement wanted by reducing the existing width F–D by the difference D–E = 6cm. Draw a new underarm curve to meet the sleeve end.

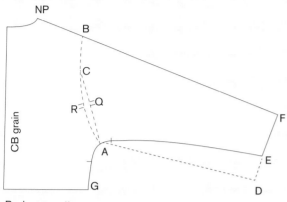

Back prep pattern
A–Q = A–R = 11cm

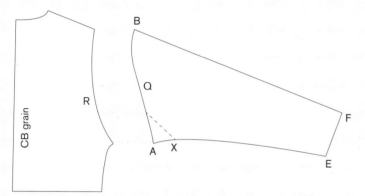

Back final pattern
A–X = 5cm

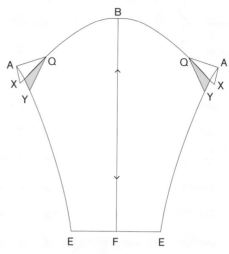

Gusset
A–X = 5cm
X–Y = 4cm

BUILT-IN GUSSET

The introduction of extra length replaces the need for a gusset to move the arm. If more movement is needed then make the slash line longer and open out more, adding more length, and taking it higher up the sleeve crown.

BACK

Follow instructions for the front, making sure the armhole lines meet at the shoulder and underarm for front and back. The front and back sleeve widths will not be the same because the shoulder line has moved forward.

SEPARATING THE BODY AND SLEEVE

1.
Separate the body and sleeve following lines A–Q–C–B for sleeve and A–R–C–B for body front and back.

2.
On new paper draw a line for centre sleeve line (B–F). Place the front and back sleeves together on the centre line B–F to reform a whole sleeve. Check the sleeve end is square to the centre line.

3.
Measure down the sleeve underarm arm seams equally front and back A–X = 5cm. From X draw a slash line to the point Q on the armhole front and back. Slash up this line to open out the underarm seam X–Y = 4cm. This adds extra length to the sleeve underarm seam and acts like a gusset.

4.
Redraw the sleeve seam A–E, curving through Y and smoothing out the line. A pattern master would help draw this line. Make sure all balance marks are transferred.

126 **Sleeves, Collars and Circles**

Sleeve fundamentals
Set-in sleeves
Grown-on sleeves
Sleeve cuffs

Collar fundamentals
One-piece collars
Two-piece collars
Circles and ruffles

SLEEVE CUFFS

4

A sleeve can be finished in a variety of ways depending on the design. A traditional shirt sleeve is finished with a cuff. Even small details such as cuffs can have real significance in a garment. A cuff could be pleated, for example, or might use bias or the weft grain of a stripe so it stands out, or it might be defined with seam piping, lace edging or a contrasting fabric, to name just a few possibilities. The size of the cuff can also be a design feature. Oversized cuffs (such as those used in Viktor and Rolf designs) or long fitted cuffs (such as a Victorian sleeve), for example, can really help to set off a design. The simplest cuff is a straight band folding back on itself. If a shaped edge or seam is required then the cuff is cut in two parts and seamed both top and bottom.

The sleeve must be adapted to the cuff. It may need to be shortened by the depth of the cuff but it is usual to have an 'overhang' of the sleeve to the cuff. The full sleeves of the 1970s had quite a lot of overhang so the sleeve drooped over a tight cuff. It is worth leaving more than you think on the sleeve hem and experiment, as it is easier to reduce during a fitting than to add on.

<u>SLEEVE CUFFS</u>

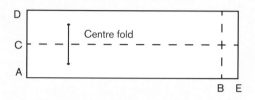
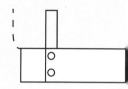

<u>Straight cuff with fold-back edge</u>

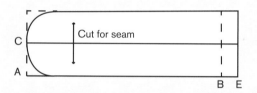
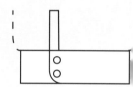

<u>Two-part seamed cuff with curved edge</u>
(The cuff is seamed as it has a curved edge).

Step-by-step

STRAIGHT CUFF WITH FOLD-BACK EDGE

1.
Draft a rectangle the length of the cuff plus button stand 1.5cm by twice the cuff depth. The length of a cuff is based on a comfortable fit on the wrist and must be large enough to allow the sleeve to move up the arm as the arm rises (18–20cm for size 10–12).
A–B = length of cuff
B–E = button extension
A–C = finished depth of cuff
A–D = double finished cuff

2.
Grain line can be on straight or weft grain as it is a small pattern.

Step-by-step

TWO-PART SEAMED CUFF WITH CURVED EDGE

1.
Draft a rectangle the length of the cuff plus button stand 1.5cm by twice the cuff depth. The width is based on a comfortable fit on the wrist and must be large enough to allow the sleeve to move up the arm as the arm rises (18–20cm size 10–12).
A–B = length of cuff
B–E = button extension
A–C = finished depth of cuff
A–D = double finished cuff

2.
Grain line can be on straight or weft grain as it is a small pattern.

3.
Fold on the centre line and draw a curve on the edge which overlaps the button stand. Trace through on the double. Cut and separate the cuff through the centre line, creating a two-part cuff.

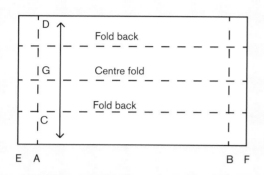

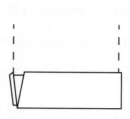

<u>One-piece straight turn-back cuff</u>
(The cuff is doubled and folded
back on itself).

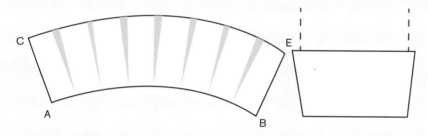

<u>Deep shaped cuff</u>
(The cuff shapes to the arm because it
is deep, becoming wider at the top).

Step-by-step

**ONE-PIECE STRAIGHT
TURN-BACK CUFF**

1.
Draft a rectangle the cuff
length plus 1.5cm added both
ends by 4 x finished cuff depth.
A–B = Cuff length
E–A and B–F = 1.5cm
extensions
A–C = finished cuff depth (fold
back line)
A–G = twice cuff depth (centre
fold line)
A–D = 2 x A–G

Step-by-step

DEEP SHAPED CUFF

1.
Draft a rectangle the length
of the cuff by depth of cuff.
A–B = length of cuff
A–C = depth of cuff

2.
Draw equally spaced parallel
slash lines from top to bottom
(A–C and A–B). This can be
done quickly by folding the
length in half then in quarters
and then eighths.

3.
Slash down these lines from
the top of the cuff and open out
each section equally to add the
required width at the top. Line
C–E will be longer than A–B.
Do not over extend the top of
the cuff as it will gape, you
want a measurement that just
clears the width of the sleeve
at the level it finishes.

128

Sleeves, Collars and Circles

Sleeve fundamentals
Set-in sleeves
Grown-on sleeves
Sleeve cuffs

Collar fundamentals
One-piece collars
Two-piece collars
Circles and ruffles

4

COLLAR FUNDAMENTALS

A collar is made up of two elements – it has a stand (if it rises at all into the neck) and a fall as it falls away from the rise (unless it is completely flat). This is an important relationship.

There are basic principles that need to be understood when drafting collars or creating them on the tailor's dummy.

- The first principle is the length of the outer edge of the collar. This will affect how it will work on the garment and body; the longer the outer length, the flatter it will lie on the body. As the outer edge shortens (is reduced), the more it will rise up into the neck. Therefore there is some trial and error in the process to get the perfect look and behaviour. Some examples are demonstrated in this chapter, and hopefully they will give you confidence to create more technically challenging collars.

- The second principle is the neckline measurement. This is used to draft collars and, because these collars are sewn into the neckline, this never changes (unless of course there are changes to the neckline shape).

- The third principle is that a one-piece collar cannot function for all collars that rise into the neck; the shorter outer edge forces the fabric up and over, creating a 'stand' into the neck. Only a certain amount of 'rise' can be tolerated before it starts to 'crack'; the collar must then be divided into the stand and the fall, so that the stand is shaped and fitted neatly to the neck and the fall drops down from the top edge of the stand.

The method of reducing the outer edge is not technically characteristic in industry but it shows how collars drafted by measurement should look, and will help to demonstrate the relationship between the stand and the fall.

When working with two-part collars, the fundamentals are:

- The stand shapes to fit the neck curve and will funnel more as it rises upward.

- If the top edge of the stand is reduced, it must also be reduced by the same amount on the stand/fall seam line.

- Generally, the fall is deeper than the stand so that it covers the seam or touches the body – depending on the shape and size.

- Before drafting the collar, it can help to gauge the potential length of the outer edge by measuring it with a flexible tape measure in the position it will take on the body – this will give you a guide.

- A collar can be slightly adjusted by either reducing or expanding it, either at the neckline or outer edge.

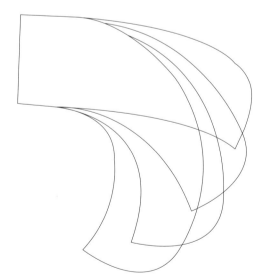

Above
Collars
The slope of the collar determines its shape and depth.

Left
<u>Kinder Aguggini AW10</u>
Collars follow their own trends
on the catwalk.

Sleeve fundamentals
Set-in sleeves
Grown-on sleeves
Sleeve cuffs

Collar fundamentals
One-piece collars
Two-piece collars
Circles and ruffles

ONE-PIECE COLLARS

4

One-piece collars are cut with the stand included.

PETER PAN COLLAR

This collar lays flat on the body and has only a 'fall' of a collar. Ideally, there should be a slight rise into the neck as this is more attractive.

PETER PAN COLLAR

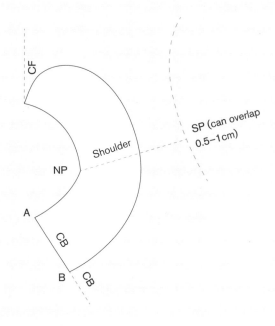

Basic Peter Pan collar
A–B = depth of collar (14cm)

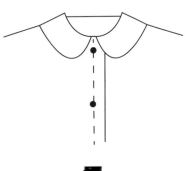

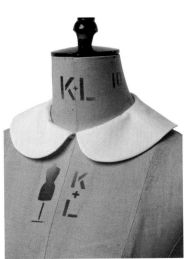

Step-by-step

1.
Prepare the pattern or block and make any adjustments to the neckline, such as lowering it slightly.

2.
Place front and back together at the shoulder line with NPs and SPs meeting. (The shoulder points can overlap 0.5–1cm). Trace off the neckline, CF and CB lines.

3.
Draw the shape of the collar as it will lie on the body, measuring equally down from the neckline. Draw a curve of the outer edge, meeting the CB at right angles. Finish the front collar in a curved shape to CF neckline point. Cut around the collar and test on the dummy or yourself. Adjust if necessary.

ETON COLLAR

Depth = stand + fall

CB

0.75cm dart

0.75cm dart

1.5cm dart

SH

Outer edge

CB

Closed dart

Closed dart

Closed dart

Outer edge

Adding the darts

Final Eton collar

This collar starts as a Peter Pan collar and rises more into the neck by reducing the outer edge with darts.

Step-by-step

1.
Follow instructions for Peter Pan collar and cut out.

2.
Create three darts on the outer edge: 1–1.5cm at the shoulder and two darts 75mm spaced equally from shoulder to CB line. Fold these darts away to nothing at the neck. This flattens the collar at the back and reduces the outer edge so that the collar is forced to rise up the neck.

3.
Retrace the collar, making good the outer and inner curves. Place CB on fold of paper and create a full collar, checking that the inner and outer curves meet the CB line at right angles. Open out and check.

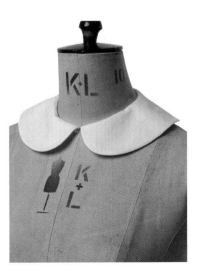

132   **Sleeves, Collars and Circles**

Sleeve fundamentals
Set-in sleeves
Grown-on sleeves
Sleeve cuffs

Collar fundamentals
One-piece collars
Two-piece collars
Circles and ruffles

4

COLLARS WITH MORE RISE I

These two collar examples use the same principle of reducing the outer edge of the flat collar to create more 'rise' into the neck and 'fall' away from the neck. Notice the relationship of the inner and outer lines as the collars become straighter. Once you become more accustomed to the behaviour of collars they can be confidently drafted by measurements, using the neck length, the depth of the collar which is the stand (rise) and fall, and the length of the outer edge as it sits on the body.

COLLAR WITH MORE RISE I

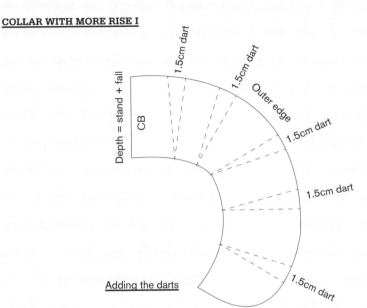

Adding the darts

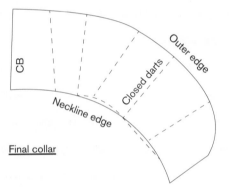

Final collar

Step-by-step

1.
Follow instructions for drafting a Peter Pan collar (see page 130). Cut out. Depth = stand + fall measurement.

2.
Create five equally spaced darts of 1.5cm each on the outer edge of the collar. Fold darts away to nothing at the neck.

3.
Redraw and make true the inner and outer curves of the collar, making sure the lines meet the CB at right angles. Check the neckline measurement is still the same and correct on CB line if necessary – either adding or reducing CB line parallel to original.

COLLAR WITH MORE RISE II

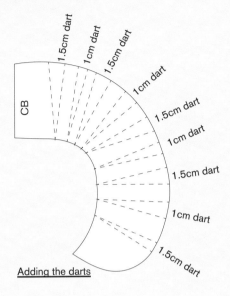

Adding the darts

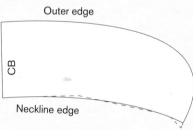

Outer edge

CB

Neckline edge

Final collar

Step-by-step

1.
Follow instructions for drawing a Peter Pan collar (see page 130). Depth = stand + fall measurement.

2.
Create five equally spaced darts of 1.5cm each on the outer edge of the collar as the previous collar. Add four more 1cm darts between these larger darts, or distribute the nine darts equally 1.27cm per dart. Fold darts away to nothing at the neck.

3.
Redraw and make true the inner and outer curves of the collar. Check the neckline measurement is still the same and correct on CB line if necessary – either adding or reducing CB line parallel to original.

COLLARS WITH MORE RISE II

The number of darts on the outer edge reduces the outer edge line to almost the same as the neckline. The pattern will at this stage have very uneven lines, so be careful not to lose any length on the neckline. This collar would work well cut on the bias of the fabric as it will curve nicely around the neck. Compare the neckline of two-piece collars and you may notice it turns up rather than down, this is because there is 'rise' all the way through the neck.

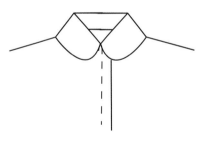

134   **Sleeves, Collars and Circles**

Sleeve fundamentals
Set-in sleeves
Grown-on sleeves
Sleeve cuffs

Collar fundamentals
One-piece collars
Two-piece collars
Circles and ruffles

4

TWO-PIECE COLLARS

A collar cut in two parts – with a stand and a fall – offers more control of the fit at the neck and how the collar will fall. Generally, the deeper the stand, the more it shapes to the neck.

Refer to page 128 for the fundamental principles of two-part collars.

SHIRT COLLAR

This classic collar can be a foundation to a variety of collars which have a stand and fall close to the neck. This collar example fits close to the neck with an extension on the stand for a button fastening. The outer edge line and fall shape can be altered to suit a variety of designs. The way the fall behaves on a garment can be adjusted by lengthening the outer edge.

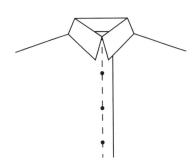

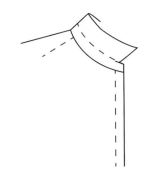

SHIRT COLLAR

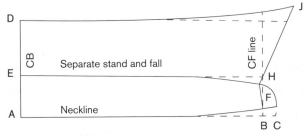

One-piece draft pattern

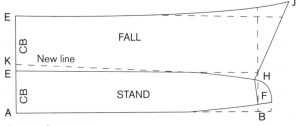

Intermediate pattern

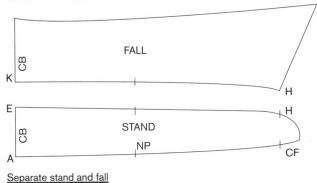

Separate stand and fall

Step-by-step

Preparation
Lower the front neckline of the block 0.5cm to 1cm. Measure the new neckline from CF–CB and make a note.

1.
Draft construction lines creating a rectangle:
length = neckline (A–B) + button stand (B–C) (1.5cm)
height = stand and fall combined (A–D) (7cm).
The squared line from B is the CF line.

2.
Measure the depth of stand from neckline up CB line A–E = 3cm. Square across to meet CF line.

3.
Mark NP on neckline. Raise point B 0.5cm to point F (B–F = 0.5cm). Draw a new neckline curving gently upwards from the straight neckline through point F to G.

4.
Square up from F on this new line 2cm to point H. From CB, connect E–H–G with the line curving downwards through H and sharply to G. Make sure the line squares to the line F–G.

5.
Draft the outer edge shape of the collar and fall from H–J, extending beyond the construction line. Mark a balance point in line with NP.

6.
Cut and separate collar along the new lines.

Note: A new line can separate E–H 0.5cm above parallel from CB (point K) and then curving to meet H. This can help the 'set' of the collar by making it fall away from the neckline slightly (see middle diagram).

HIGH-STAND COLLAR

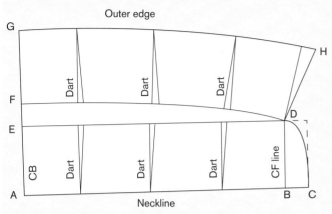

Adding the darts

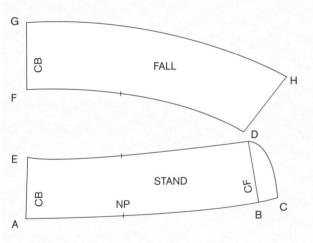

Final collar

HIGH-STAND COLLAR

This collar example has a high stand, which needs to be fitted as it rises into the neck. In the draft the relationship between the stand and the fall changes as it rises higher into the neck and the stand needs to be shaped to fit. The outer edge of the collar can be increased by slashing equidistant lines from the outer edge to seam line and adding length on the outer edge. The drafting of the collar depends on the design.

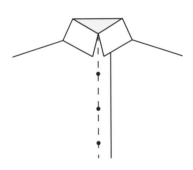

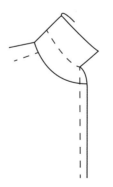

Step-by-step

Preparation
Draft the stand as a rectangle length = neckline (A–B) + button stand (B–C) (1.5cm) height = stand (A–E) (4.5cm). Square the CF line up from B to D. Connect D–C with a sharp curve, taking off the corner. Mark NP balance on neckline.

1.
Extend CB line above E the depth of stand plus 1cm, plus 1.5cm to G (A–G = 6.5cm). On this line F is 1.5cm (E–F = 1.5cm).

2.
Draw line F–D square to CB line from F, then curving gently to meet D at CF line.

3.
Draw the outer edge of the collar from G–H equidistant from line F–D (5cm). Extend the collar edge to a desired shape.

4.
On line A–B draw three evenly distributed darts of 0.25cm deep from top edge, one in the back and two in the front.

5.
Draw the same size and position of darts as the stand on line F–D. Mark balance points.

6.
Cut out the stand and fall. Fold the darts away in the stand from top to neckline edge, and from seam to outer edge on the fall. Redraw the new shapes.

Note: The outer edge of the fall can be adjusted by slashing equally spaced lines down to the seam and adding extra length. This is more likely if the fall of the collar is big.

136

Sleeves, Collars and Circles

Sleeve fundamentals
Set-in sleeves
Grown-on sleeves
Sleeve cuffs

Collar fundamentals
One-piece collars
Two-piece collars
Circles and ruffles

CIRCLES AND RUFFLES

4

Circle patterns are effective in creating full ruffles at the neck and cuff and cascading ruffles. The weight and thickness of cloth and depth of ruffles will determine the size and shape of these patterns. The more circles you add, the more ruffles will be created. The case study on the opposite page would need several circles to achieve such fullness. It is helpful to test the fabric and circle ratios in cloth so that you can establish how many circles you may need and how deep. The grain of the circles varies from straight to bias, and where you position the grain will influence the way it falls and the look.

CIRCLES AND RUFFLES

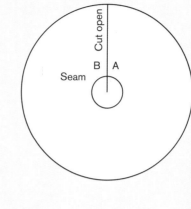

Full ruffles
A–B = length of seam to be inserted or section of seam.
Inside circle is seam line, outside circle is hem.

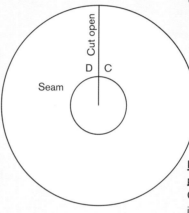

Less full ruffles or gathered/ pleated finish
C–D = length of seam to be inserted for less full ruffles.
Inside circle is seam line, outside circle is hem.

Step-by-step

Radius = circumference divided by 6.28.

1.
Measure the length of the seam the ruffles will be inserted into (C–D = seam length or part of).

If more circles are required, divide the length of the seam line equally so that the circles will fit comfortably. You can allow a little extra length if there are a few circles as the seams may be tight and may pull when sewn.

If gathers or pleats are required, do a test in fabric first to establish how much extra to add. Then create your circles according to the extra length needed for the gathering.

[Case study]
Nadine Mukhtar

Nadine's work has been inspired by radial spirals and geometric forms. The fan shapes radiate around the body in 3D. Circles are used to create a full ruffled effect at the neckline in the jacket.

Technical flat drawings of Nadine's collection

Sketchbook pages

Nadine's final garments

5

TROUSERS

Pattern cutters can also set trends with trousers. Altering the waist or crotch height, adding pleats and widening the hem can all change the shape and fit – and, if used creatively, can create iconic designs.

140 Trouser fundamentals

142 Standard fit

144 Adding pleats

148 Above-waist fitting

152 Below-waist fitting

156 Pockets, zips and finishes

Trouser fundamentals
Standard fit
Adding pleats
Above-waist fitting
Below-waist fitting
Pockets, zips and finishes

TROUSER FUNDAMENTALS

The idea that women were once 'not allowed' to wear trousers seems ridiculous now. Although women began to wear trousers early on in the twentieth century, it was really Yves Saint Laurent who made trousers chic and highly fashionable, along with his reworking of 'the smoking jacket'. Trousers were the domain of male attire, as much as skirts were the domain of female attire. In particular, this gendering of clothing was somewhat erased when jeans were adopted by men and women alike. Jeans also eroded to some degree the notion of 'class' as everyone could wear jeans for informal occasions. The separating of 'workwear' and 'leisurewear' has lessened, and trousers have a place in any modern wardrobe.

Designers such as Vivienne Westwood have created iconic trousers in more recent years. Her punk, bondage-style strapped trousers, and her pirate trousers, which were created without a CF seam, thus creating large volumes of fabric at the crotch, are some of her best-known creations.

Alexander McQueen also redefined the trouser, with his bottom-revealing 'bumster' trousers. This at the time was seen as a dangerous and rebellious fashion move:

'With bumsters I wanted to elongate the body, not just show the bum. To me, that part of the body – not so much the buttocks, but the bottom and the spine – that is the most erotic part of anyone's body, man or woman.'

Fashion shapes and fit change: from the deep-crotch hip-hop trouser, twisted seam jeans that distort the leg shape, to jodphurs that fit the calves and have width at the buttocks, and harem pants that are voluminous and gathered at the hem.

This chapter introduces some common trouser fundamentals. It demonstrates the differences between narrow-leg and wide-leg trousers, and how to adapt basic blocks to achieve some simple design features with pleats and pockets, including fitting below the waist and raising above the waist.

Elsa Schiaperelli
Of course we don't want pants!

Left
<u>Balenciaga SS12</u>
Trouser shapes and fit change.
Deep-crotch, high-waist,
wide-hem – all have a place on
the catwalk!

142   **Trousers**

Trouser fundamentals
Standard fit
Adding pleats
Above-waist fitting
Below-waist fitting
Pockets, zips and finishes

5

STANDARD FIT

In any trouser block or pattern, it is important to note the relationship of front and back, and how the back crotch line is much longer than the front. The reason for this is because a short front crotch line does not 'drag' the fabric backwards, thus allowing it to lie flatter. The length of this line is crucial in fitting. The back crotch line also dips below the front crotch level in the pattern construction, which shortens the inside leg slightly. This is then compensated for by 'stretching' the back inside leg between the notches to the front inside leg when sewing together.

Generally the back waist has two darts to distribute the shaping over the buttocks.

The width of the leg should be determined by the design but remember that the foot will need to go through so you'll need to allow about 32cm at the hem for this.

The grain line is important so as not to twist when being worn – generally, it is square to the crotch line. Adjustments can be made at the fitting stage if out of alignment. Usually, this is just a case of lifting or dropping the side seam line, unless there are more serious fitting issues.

The front waist has a dart which allows for a shaped fit, but it can be removed for a flatter fit (generally in younger ranges and jeans) by distributing the excess at the side seam and CF line.

MEASURING FOR A TROUSER BLOCK (RECAP)

The following are measured:

- Waist (as bodice).
- Hip (as skirt).
- Top hip (as skirt).

- Outside leg.
- Inside leg.

- Body rise – IMPORTANT measurement – the length of the body from waist to level surface when seated. Note: Use a ruler, set square or rigid rule and measure at the side.

For high-waist trousers or skirts, measure above waist. For low-waist trousers, measure at the level wanted.

**BASIC STANDARD FIT
TROUSERS**

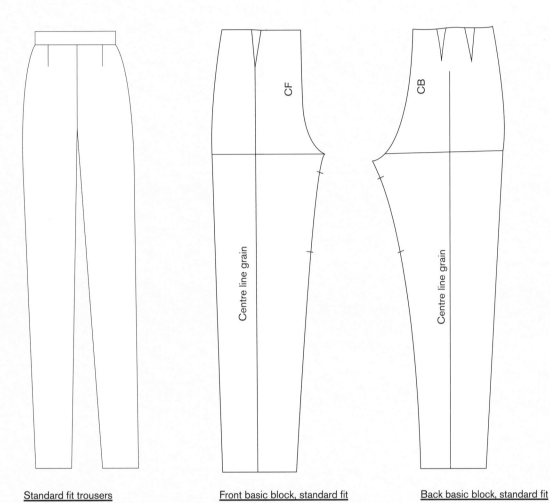

Standard fit trousers   Front basic block, standard fit   Back basic block, standard fit

Trouser fundamentals
Standard fit
Adding pleats
Above-waist fitting
Below-waist fitting
Pockets, zips and finishes

ADDING PLEATS

5

The technique of adding pleats to a pattern can be used in a variety of circumstances, such as in skirts and sleeves. The examples here show how to introduce a pleat that is located in a specific area and not all the way through a garment. The examples on pages 146–147 have pleats added all the way through the garment. The pleat is usually placed so that it folds (creases) towards the side seam from the centre line and includes the dart width, so depending on how much pleat is required the pattern will spread as needed. Always do a test in fabric or at least paper to get a sense of the depth of the pleat you want. The centre line is often referred to as the crease line.

ADDING PLEATS WITH NO CHANGE TO THE HEM

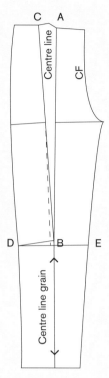

Adding the pleats
A–B = 66–68cm
A–C = 5cm (to include waist dart)

Step-by-step

This example introduces a pleat at the waist but it does not widen the hem.

FRONT

1.
Trace around the basic block front, marking in the crotch line, centre line (grain line) all the way to the waist and dart. Move the dart so that it begins from the CF side of the centre line.

2.
Mark a position where the pleat will end (A–B = 66–68cm). Square a line across at this level. Cut out around block.

3.
Cut down the centre line A–B and across to D and E. Lay on new paper and open the waist for a pleat to include the waist dart (C–A = 5cm). Fold the pleat on the centre line nearest the waist and trace through for the new waistline. Redraw and make true all lines, marking in grain line.

BACK

Use the standard trouser back block as there has been no change to the hem width.

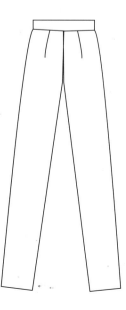

ADDING A PLEAT ALL THE WAY TO THE HEM

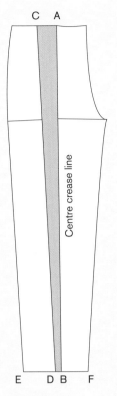

Prep pattern

A–C = 6cm (to include waist dart)

D–B = 1.5cm

Final patterns

Step-by-step

This example demonstrates how to introduce a wider pleat at the waist all the way to the hem. Extra width can be added to the hem, as the example shows, and the whole fit is wider on the body.

FRONT

1.
Use a standard-fit block and trace around the front, marking all relevant darts, crotch line level, grain line and balance marks. Make any adjustments to the waist level if necessary. Cut around block.

2.
Lay onto new paper. Decide where the position of the pleat will be – generally, it is from the centre line (crease line) towards the side so that the CF area stays on grain. Move waist dart along the waistline towards the side seam so that it becomes incorporated in the pleat.

3.
Cut along the centre line A–B and separate. Open A–C to create pleat (A–C = 6cm and includes dart) and add a small amount of width at the hem (D–B = 1.5cm). The additional width will throw the crotch level off as it swings open for the pleat. This is ok if the hem is kept relatively level. Make sure the centre line is marked in.

4.
Add extra width at the hem equally either side on inside (F) and outside seams (E) (2cm each side in this example). Draw straight lines to meet the curve at the hip on the side seam and gently curve the inner leg seam toward the inner leg top. Measure the inside leg.

5.
Fold the upper section of the pleat closed and trace through the shape it makes at the waist.

BACK

1.
Use a standard-fit block and trace around the back, marking all relevant darts, crotch line, and centre line (grain line). Make any adjustments to the waistline if necessary. Do not cut out yet.

2.
Add together the additional front hem width to calculate the back hem width. Divide the sum in two (2.8cm in this example) and add to either side of the back hem (G + 2.8cm and H + 2.8cm). Draw a straight line from H to meet the curve of the hip on the side seam and gently curve the inner leg seam from G towards the top of the inner leg.

Check the outer side lengths are the same, and the inner leg seams match between notches. Adjust if necessary.

Trouser fundamentals
Standard fit
Adding pleats
Above-waist fitting
Below-waist fitting
Pockets, zips and finishes

5

WIDE LEG WITH ONE PLEAT

The pattern demonstrates an increase of width through the whole front leg with a pleat and straight outside and inside seams squared to the hem. The look is much looser and with the extra width in the back it hangs loosely over the buttocks.

WIDE STRAIGHT LEG WITH ONE PLEAT

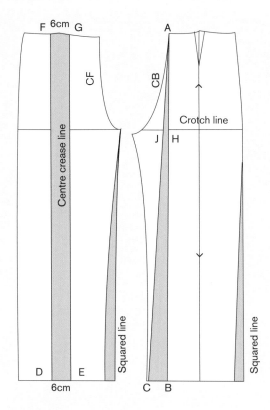

Adding the pleat
D–E = 6cm
C–B = 5.6cm

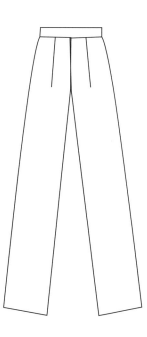

Step-by-step

FRONT

1.
Follow instructions for adding a pleat all the way to the hem, but add the same width of pleat all the way through to the hem (D–E = 6cm and F–G = 6cm).

2.
Add extra width at the hem by squaring the side seam to the hem and inside leg. The side seam line will meet the hip curve and the inner leg seam will gently curve to the top. Transfer balance marks on inner leg and measure line.

3.
Fold the upper part of the pleat on centre (crease) line at the waist closed and trace through the shape.

BACK

1.
Trace around back basic trouser block, marking in all relevant darts, crotch line, centre line and balance marks. Cut out around block.

2.
Draw a line A–B square to the crotch line. Cut up this line from B–A, but do not cut completely off. Lay the pattern on new paper and open out at hem (C–B = 5.6cm) to add width so that the hem forms a square to the inside leg seam line.

3.
Square the side seam to the hem in a straight line to meet the hip curve, this adds hem width, but it will not necessarily be equal to the inserted width on the inside leg.

Check the outer side lengths are the same, and the inner leg seams match between notches. Adjust if necessary.

EXTRA WIDE LEG WITH TWO PLEATS

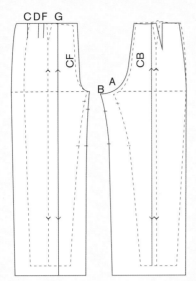

C D F G

Prep pattern
A–B = 4cm
G–F = 6cm (pleat)
D–F = 2cm (gap)
D–C = 4.8cm (pleat)

Final pattern
A–B = 4cm
G–F = 6cm (pleat)
D–F = 2cm (gap)
D–C = 4.8cm (pleat)

EXTRA WIDE LEG WITH TWO PLEATS

These trousers are more commonly known as 'Oxford bags'. They are roomy with extra width at crotch level on the inside leg. The CF line can be almost square to the crotch line and sits lower than normal. See the comparison diagram.

Step-by-step

Preparation
Follow instructions for the wide straight leg with one pleat.

FRONT

1.
Straighten the CF line square to the crotch line, this will add width to the waist.

2.
Along the waistline mark the additional pleat 2cm toward the side seam (F–D = 2cm). Move the whole pattern outward keeping it level on the crotch line to add an extra pleat (D–C = 4.8cm). The leg is now widened through.

3.
Complete the tracing of the pattern with the pleats folded away at the waist.

BACK

1.
Extend the crotch line beyond the existing inside seam line (A–B = 4cm), flattening it out parallel to the crotch line. This adds extra width between the front and back crotch.

2.
Follow the existing shape of the inside line now 4cm extra, making sure it is still square to the hem.

3.
Optional: Move the back waist dart over slightly and slant toward the side seam, keeping the same size and length. This helps to get a better line for a back pocket.

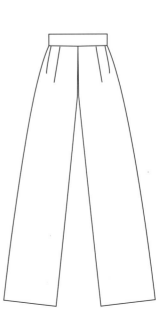

Trouser fundamentals
Standard fit
Adding pleats
Above-waist fitting
Below-waist fitting
Pockets, zips and finishes

ABOVE-WAIST FITTING

Elongating the leg by extending above the waist and changing upper proportions has been popular several times in the 1930s–1940s, 1980s–1990s and 2010–2011. It can be flattering and comfortable as it sits against the body above the waist. There is a limit to how high the extension can be before boning is needed to hold it up, and this can depend on the fabric and interfacing.

'GROWN-ON' WAISTBAND

This example has the waistband 'grown-on', as the trouser extends above the waist. Ideally, the top of the extension will fit closely so a body measurement is needed at the level it finishes. The number of waist darts can be increased to distribute the shaping, particularly in the back.

'GROWN-ON' WAISTBAND

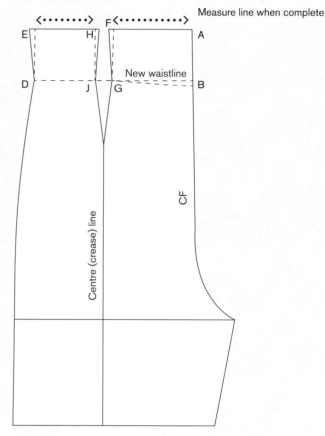

Front pattern
A–B = 6cm
D–E = 6cm
F–G = H–J = 6cm

Step-by-step

FRONT

1.
Trace around the basic front block, marking in the dart, centre line (grain line) and crotch level line. Make sure there is enough paper above the waist for the 'grown-on' waistband.

2.
Square a new waistline across from CF line. From this new waistline square up B–A the depth of the waistband extension (6cm).

3.
Square construction lines up from the new waistline from each side of the dart and side seam. Reduce the fitting of the dart above the waist (G–F = 6cm) (J–H = 6cm) and increase at side seam (D–E = 6cm). Draw new lines above the waist. (See note on calculating fitting.)

4.
Draw in top edge with a line square to CF across to the side seam. Adjust this line by folding the dart closed from the top to waist and making good the curve of the top line. Measure the line to make sure it is correct.

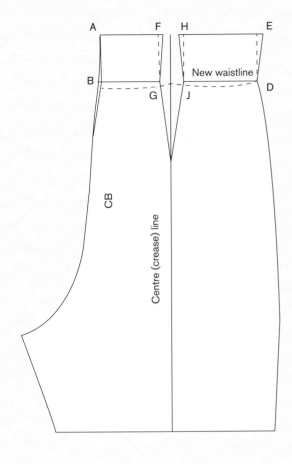

BACK

1.
Trace around the basic back block, marking in the dart, centre line (grain line) and crotch level line. Make sure there is enough paper above the waist for the 'grown-on' waistband.

2.
Square a new waistline across from side seam. From this new waistline square up B–A the depth of the waistband extension (6cm).

3.
Square construction lines up from the new waistline from each side of the dart and side seam. Reduce the fitting of the dart above the waist (G–F = 6cm) (J–H = 6cm) and increase at side seam (D–E = 6cm). Draw new lines above the waist. (See note on calculating fitting.)

4.
Draw in top edge with a line square to CB across to the side seam. Adjust this line by folding the dart closed from the top to waist and making good the curve of the top line. Measure the line to make sure it is correct.

CALCULATING THE FIT ABOVE THE WAIST

1. The bodice block can be used to calculate the width above the waist, but it must be reduced for a tight fit, (i.e. remove all ease added to the pattern).

2. Use the standard measurement charts.

3. Measure a tailor's dummy.

4. Measure a person.

Once an overall measurement is established, calculate the distribution of shaping by the difference of the actual width on the pattern before adjusting to the required width. Divide this equally between the darts and side seams.

A fitting will help to resolve any problems, and will also give a good indication of whether boning would be required.

Usually, the waist extension is finished with a facing, and if boned it needs to reach the waist.

150   Trousers

Trouser fundamentals
Standard fit
Adding pleats
Above-waist fitting
Below-waist fitting
Pockets, zips and finishes

5

TIGHTER FIT TROUSER/JEANS

Trousers that fit close to the body need a longer back crotch line. This example is preparation for a jean pattern, with no front waist dart. If a very tight fit is desired then it is preferable to use a fabric with stretch in it, and to reduce the pattern through the centre line. It is best to do a stretch test with the fabric and then calculate the percentage of stretch and adjust from that. If the ankle is very tight and there is no stretch in the fabric then a zip, popper, button or lacing opening is needed. Alternatively, the design could include a stretch inset or an interesting way to allow the foot to go through the hem. Although the pattern preparation is for a jean pattern, it must be noted that good jean patterns and fit are a specialist area within pattern cutting.

Before stretch fabrics, jean patterns were often cut larger, shrunk to size and then refitted. In the 1960s and 1970s, jeans were shrunk on the body by sitting in a bath of hot water! Stretch gives the jeans a tight fit without fear of splitting seams open when sitting down or from general use. The main disadvantage of stretch jeans is that they can drag down, this is because the body warms the fabric and it stretches more around the body than the leg.

TIGHTER FIT TROUSER/JEANS

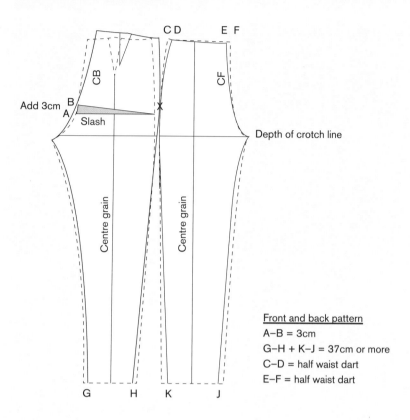

Front and back pattern
A–B = 3cm
G–H + K–J = 37cm or more
C–D = half waist dart
E–F = half waist dart

Step-by-step

1.
Trace around front and back basic trouser block, keeping level at the crotch line.

2.
Back: Draw a line across from A on CB line 6cm above and parallel to the crotch line to side seam X.

3.
Slash and spread at A to add 3cm extra CB length. This will change the angle of the waist. Redraw on new paper, making good the curve on CB line.

4.
Front: Remove the waist dart by distributing the measurement of the dart equally at the CF line and side seam (C–D and E–F). This will increase the slope on the CF line. If it looks too much (depending on body size), then adjust so that more is taken at the side seam. Redraw the waistline in a curve which meets the CF and side seam at right angles.

5.
Front and back: Slim the legs by reducing the outer edges equally, so that with non-stretch fabric the hem width is no less than 37cm. Redraw the inside legs, hollowing out the line around the inner thigh area. Mark balance points 6cm from the top and 54cm from the hem.

6.
Adjust/reduce hip width if necessary.

ADDING A BACK YOKE
(low-waist example)

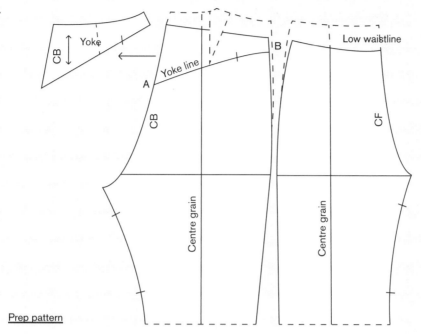

Prep pattern

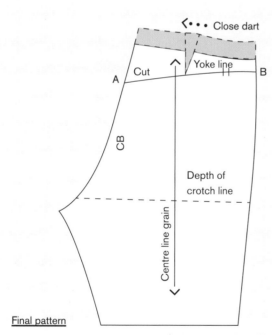

Final pattern

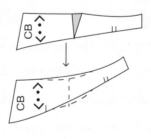

BACK YOKE

The same method is used to create a yoke for a standard-waist-fit jean or trouser.

Step-by-step

1.
Trace off a back block, in this example the low-waist trouser/jean block.

2.
Close the waist dart and draw a curved line from a point down CB (A) to a point on side seam (B), with the line touching the end of the waist dart. This will be the size and shape of the yoke.

3.
Mark balance marks and then cut along A–B to separate yoke from lower trouser.

4.
The waist dart is kept closed and the shaping moves to the seam. Draw new curves for the seam and waist to remove any awkward shapes made by the closed dart.

Trouser fundamentals
Standard fit
Adding pleats
Above-waist fitting
Below-waist fitting
Pockets, zips and finishes

5

BELOW-WAIST FITTING

A low-waist trouser will need to fit well at the level it sits so accurate measurement and fitting is needed. In many cases if the waist is too low and the waistband not shaped enough, the CB can gape. A hollow back or proportionally larger buttock to waist is best cut with a waistband that is higher at the CB than CF. The waistband must be cut from the existing pattern so it will curve to fit the shape of the body.

<u>LOW-WAIST TROUSER</u>

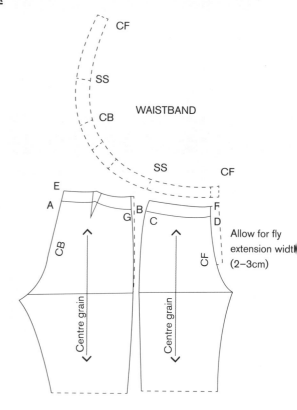

Step-by-step

1.
Front and back: Trace front and back jeans pattern, marking the centre line, crotch line, back dart and balance marks.

2.
Measure down from the waist to where the new waist will be, either equidistant or shaped from a higher CB. Draw a curved line from CB to side seam (A–B) and CF to side seam (E–D).

BACK

1.
Adjust the length of A–B on the body by removing the dart and taking the width of the small dart off at the side. Reshape the side seam to meet this new point (G). This is not advisable if the buttock is proportionally larger than the waist – in this case keep the dart where it is.

2.
Mark balance points along the waistband seam, making sure they match when the dart is removed (see diagram close-up).

3.
Separate the waistband along the seam line, close the waist dart and redraw.

FRONT

1.
Draw a zip extension (2–3cm) on the pattern parallel to CF, keeping the waist curve, and squaring it to the extension line and curving it down to a point approx 2cm below the end of the zip. This extension will be traced off separately and used for a fly front (see separate section on fly front).

2.
Mark balance points along the waistband seam line. Cut and separate the waistband to include the zip extension.

LOW WAISTBAND

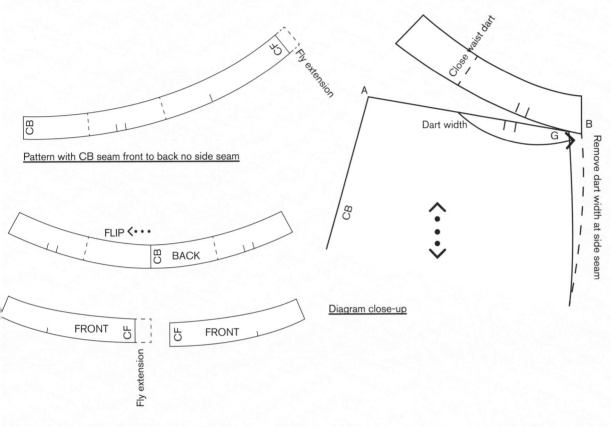

Pattern with CB seam front to back no side seam

FLIP ‹ • • •

CB BACK

Pattern with side seams

FRONT CF

CF FRONT

Fly extension

Close waist dart

A

Dart width

G

B

CB

Remove dart width at side seam

Diagram close-up

Step-by-step

PATTERN IN SECTIONS

Joins can be made at CB or at side seams, depending on the design and fabric costing.

CB seam: With a CB seam, place the front and back side seams together. Trace through on double paper, transferring balance marks so there are two sides. Mark the CF extension on the side that matches the trouser, but not both ends.

Grain line: Usually, the CF is on straight grain.

Side seam: Place the CB along the edge of folded paper. Trace through the waistband lines to the side seam, and add balance marks. Place front onto double paper (but not on fold), trace through waistband lines to side seam, add balance marks. Make sure the CF extension is on the correct side, and on only one side.

Grain line: CB fold and CF will be on straight grain.

Note: The waistband can be cut as one piece, but in industry it is likely to be separated for better costing, using CB fold as grain line.

PATTERN AS ONE PIECE

Join the F and B at the side seam. Place the CB on edge of folded paper (to copy for the other side), and pin carefully to avoid paper slip. Trace front and back waistband including balance marks and side seam position through to include under paper. Mark extension width one side only.

154   **Trousers**

Trouser fundamentals
Standard fit
Adding pleats
Above-waist fitting
Below-waist fitting
Pockets, zips and finishes

5

TROUBLESHOOTING

Trousers can be easy or difficult to fit depending on the design and the body of the person wearing them. Generally, wider trousers are easier as they fall away from legs. Tight trousers, which are close to the body and legs, can create problems at the crotch. In any event, it is desirable to have no creases at the crotch, and for the trouser to centre in the middle of the leg.

Fitting can be difficult as there are so many variables. It helps, however, to always make sure there is sufficient 'depth of crotch' distance between the waist and base of crotch. Low-waist trousers also still work from this relationship.

A lot of issues can also be resolved by realigning the side seams.

Always make sure the grain line and crotch line are drawn on the pattern. Keep the crotch line through the centre.

Common problems
- Creasing at crotch area in front.
- Drag and gape at the back along the crotch seam.
- Twisting at the side seam.
- Twisting through the centre.
- Drag below the buttocks.

STRETCH
A trouser pattern often 'stretches' the back inside line to the front around the top thigh level – this is due to the relationship of the inside seam curves.

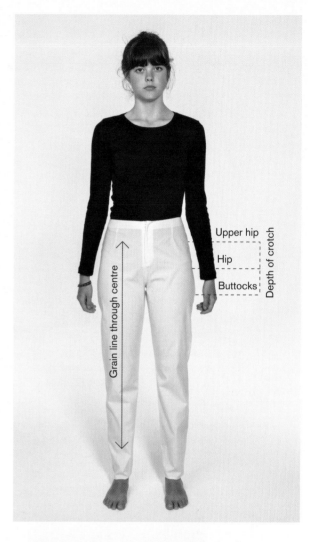

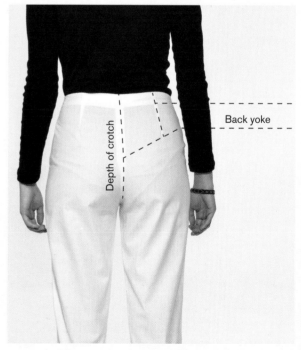

CREASING AT CROTCH AREA IN FRONT

- Check the angle of the CF crotch line, you may need more or less angle.
- Check the relationship between front and back crotch length, the front should be much shorter.
- The crotch line may need scooping (hollowing out) where the creasing is.

DRAG AND GAPE AT THE BACK ALONG THE CROTCH SEAM

- Check the length of the whole crotch line, and increase back by slashing and spreading out the difference to add length on back crotch line (as in jeans preparation).
- Reduce at waist on back crotch line if the person has a hollow back or proportionally bigger buttocks. If too long, then reduce with a dart (on the pattern).

TWISTING AT THE SIDE SEAM

- Check the front and back hems are together by overlaying them. The back should be wider than the front, this may need rebalancing.
- Check the grain lines on front and back. The grain should generally be square to the crotch line and hem.
- Check the hip width is adequate. If too tight, it can prevent the seams from lying correctly.

TWISTING THROUGH THE CENTRE

- Check the grain lines in front and back. The grain line should generally be square to the crotch line and run through the centre of the leg.
- Check side seam lengths and balance. If one length is different, keep the balance of the trouser at crotch level and adjust either side of this line.

DRAG BELOW THE BUTTOCKS

- Check the crotch line is not too short, lengthen if necessary. This can be done by adding to the underneath section of the back crotch line.
- Check that the crotch line does not need scooping (hollowing) out.
- Check that the lower leg is not too tight. Increase the calf width to allow the fabric to move.

156   **Trousers**   Trouser fundamentals
Standard fit
Adding pleats
Above-waist fitting
Below-waist fitting
Pockets, zips and finishes

POCKETS, ZIPS AND FINISHES

5

Listed here are some of the most commonly found methods for finishing off a pair of trousers.

FRONT JEANS POCKET

A key feature of this pocket is deciding on shape and depth, and where the pocket bag will be secured, at the waistline or CF line. Securing the pocket bag stops it from dislodging and twisting. If in doubt check and see how other pockets are cut and made; this helps to understand what parts make up a pocket pattern.

FRONT JEANS POCKET

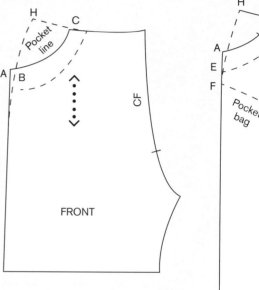

Pattern close-up

Step-by-step

1.
Draw a finished pocket line curving from waist to side seam (C–B), using a pattern master or freehand. Extend the line beyond the side seam 0.25–0.5cm to A, depending on the thickness of the fabric, to allow for the hand to enter the pocket comfortably.

2.
Draw the pocket bag shape and secure position at waist and CF (F–G). A shallow pocket may not need to reach the CF line, but a deep pocket should.

3.
Draw a line following the pocket curve approximately 3cm below (E–D). This is the side body section. You are now ready to trace off the sections for the whole pocket.

4.
Trace off the pocket that forms the underside of the pocket and side body (H–F, F–G, waist and CF lines).

5.
Trace separate piece body section (H–E, E–D, H–D). Line E–D separates the fabric from the pocket lining. In industry this piece cut in fabric is laid on top of the pocket bag and stitched down. The pocket lining below E–D can be cut separately.

6.
For the upper pocket bag lining, trace the pocket line with the new extended side (A–B–C) and the whole pocket bag below this line. Mark a balance point on the pocket line for jean and lining.

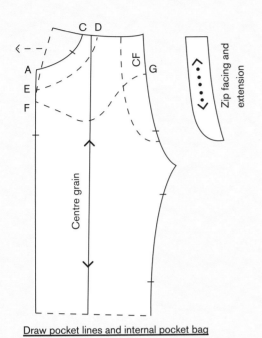

Draw pocket lines and internal pocket bag

Zip facing and extension

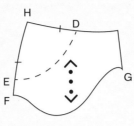

Pocket bag

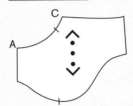

Side body section

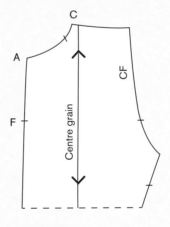

Pocket bag facing

Trouser body

7.
Erase the side body pocket
section from the pattern or
cut along the pocket line
to separate for the trouser
pattern. Mark all relevant
balance marks.

Optional: The fly front facing
and extension can be plotted
(see diagram).

158   **Trousers**   Trouser fundamentals

Standard fit

Adding pleats

Above-waist fitting

Below-waist fitting

Pockets, zips and finishes

5

'GROWN-ON' SIDE SEAM POCKETS

This type of pocket is used in a variety of situations with an extension of the side seam of the garment forming part of the pocket bag facing.

'GROWN-ON' SIDE SEAM POCKETS

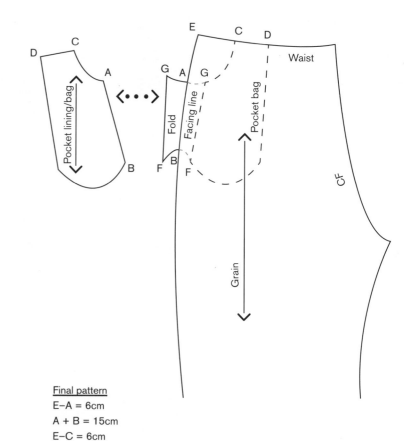

Final pattern

E–A = 6cm

A + B = 15cm

E–C = 6cm

C–D = 6cm

Step-by-step

FRONT

1.
Allow extra paper along the side seam. On side seam mark a position of the opening on the straightest section of seam from E to A (6cm). Opening line A–B is long enough to allow hand to go through (15cm). Connect these two points with a straight line (A–B).

2.
From points A and B draw the size and shape of the pocket big enough for a hand. Finish pocket at waist (C and D).

3.
Facing: Draw a diagonal line (F–G) inward from the side seam (A–B), approx 2.5–3cm deep. Fold back along A–B, and trace through the pocket facing shape. Mark balance points. Unfold the paper to flat. Line A–G, G–F and F–B becomes the facing extension, which is turned back when made.

4.
The pocket lining is traced from F–G, G–C, C–D and F–D.

BACK

Match the pattern shape at the side seam and pocket lining as for the front.

Note: It is usual to interface the facing so a separate pattern must be copied of the facing.

FLY FRONT ZIP OPENING

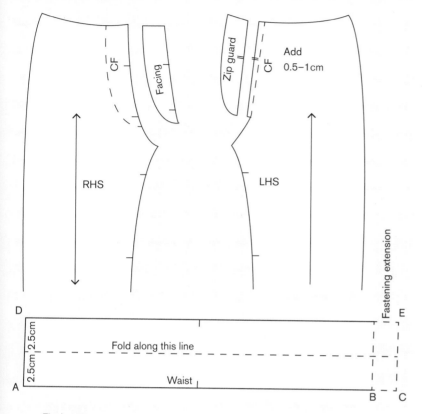

Final pattern

E–A = 6cm

A + B = 15cm

E–C = 6cm

C–D = 6cm

FLY FRONT ZIP OPENING

A fly front has two or three pattern pieces: one or two for the fly extension and one for the fly facing. The fly extension must match the waistband extension in size.

Step-by-step

1.
Mark length of zip down CF line. On front pattern draw a line parallel to CF approximately 3cm wide, extending beyond the zip end 1.5cm and curving back to CF line.

2.
Trace off three copies of the shape, marking in grain line to match CF. One copy will be for the facing and two for the fly extension.

3.
Decide which side of the CF the zip facing will finish (left or right). Label the patterns accordingly for RSU (right side up) or WSU (wrong side up) of fabric.

4.
Draft a rectangle twice the finished depth by the length of the waist. Add a button/fastening extension. Use a set square to create accurate right angles.

A–B = waist measurement of garment

B–C = extension (1.5cm)

A–D = twice finished depth (5cm)

C–E = A–D

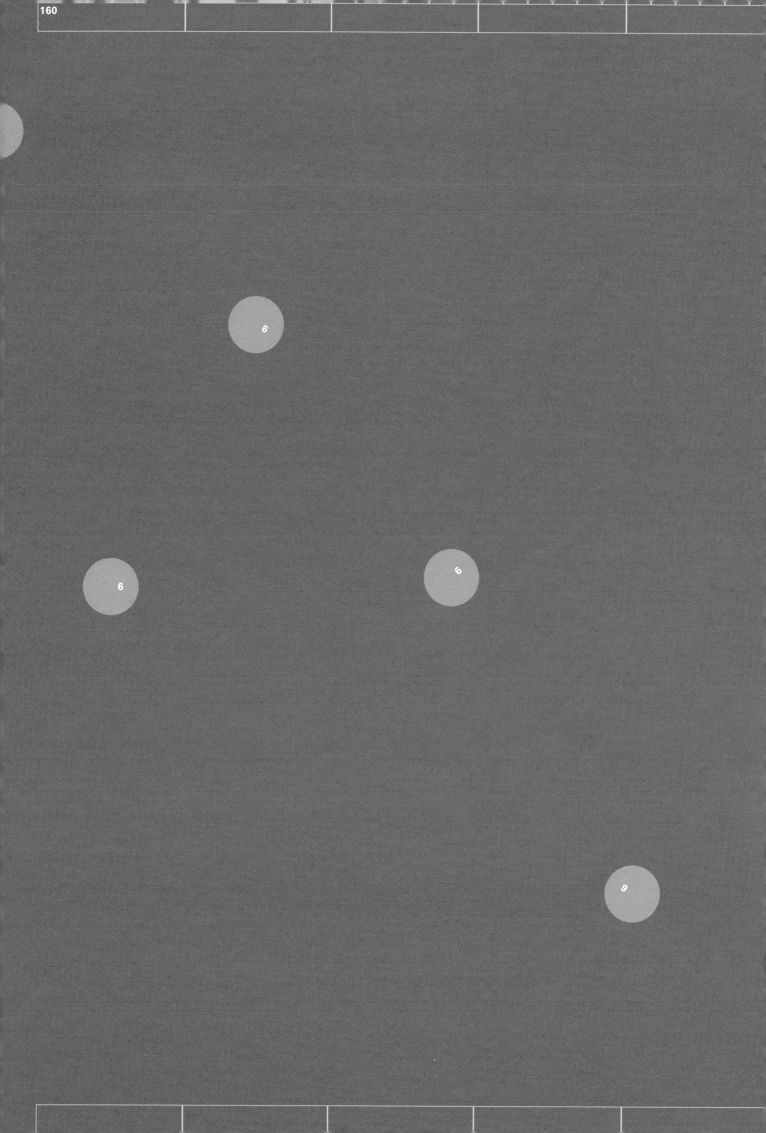

SUSTAINABILITY AND FASHION

Sustainability is now a major concern for fashion designers and pattern cutters. This chapter investigates some of the key issues affecting fashion design and showcases new methods for more sustainable and less wasteful pattern cutting.

162 Deconstructing hierarchies
and traditions
164 Pattern cutting and waste
166 New horizons

162   Sustainability and   Deconstructing hierarchies
       Fashion   and traditions
                             Pattern cutting and waste
                             New horizons

6 DECONSTRUCTING HIERARCHIES AND TRADITIONS

We presently face much debate about the depletion of the earth's resources, and issues such as 'peak oil', and the consequences of global warming. Whatever the truth, we cannot blindly continue without considering ways to minimize the impact we are making on the earth.

CONSUMPTION AND WASTE

As humans, we all need to be clothed, but we could easily live without having to choose what to wear each day. With choice comes waste, and given that 90 per cent of the resources we take from the environment now becomes waste within three months, there is a real cause for concern.

Theories as to why we humans have developed materialistic behaviour have been well debated and the marketing of products – and especially fashion – exploits this behaviour. Designer, academic and theorist Jonathan Chapman, author of *Emotionally Durable Design: Objects, Experiences and Empathy*, suggests there has been a long history of attachments to objects. Even in early civilization, for example, values were attributed to objects such as healing stones and sacred feathers; owners of such objects became empowered. Perhaps, in a similar way, owning a Prada handbag suggests 'inside' knowledge of fashion trends, and denotes some kind of superiority and empowerment.

An explosion in mass-consumerism in the Western world followed the Industrial Revolution of the nineteenth century. Society moved away from a collective, 'spiritual' sense of community to a more individualist materialism and ownership of goods. In the 1950s postmodernist era, this meant the 'function' of an object was replaced with its 'meaning', and products became symbols, icons and signs that are extensions and representations of ourselves.

Carlo Petrini

There are embedded hierarchies and systems which need to be addressed, it requires seeing things differently, shifting emphasis from the reasons and way we consume to newer models of behaviour. At the core of sustainability is a requirement that we make our systems of wealth creation less dependent on resource use, and re-calculate our relationship with speed of consumption.

AESTHETICS AND DESIGN

Richard Heinberg states in *Peak Everything: Waking Up to the Century of Declines* that 'during the twentieth century, even the noblest of industrial designers yielded products that were expressions of a system whose overall characteristics were dictated by scale, speed, accumulation and efficiency'. In the 1950s, Vance Packard wrote about 'The Waste Makers', introducing the concept of products having 'planned obsolescence'. Products and particularly fashion clothing have embedded obsolescence; they will not necessarily be unusable but they will be out of date in fashion terms. This may have been considered 'good' for the fashion industry as every season or interseason required new fashionable clothing.

In addition, population growth, travel and communication fostered innovation possibly due to exchange of ideas, competition and social change; and through innovation Western culture has been able to cut out many labour intensive tasks by creating specialized tools for these tasks, thus affording us more time for experimentation and creativity. Fashion offers an opportunity to constantly reinvent oneself through idealistic views of cultural shifts and meanings. This reinvention is playful as well as loaded with expectations, whether it is to exploit sexuality or social position.

DESIGN INTEGRITY

Richard Heinberg's opinion is that there has been a degradation of aesthetics and that we cannot be aesthetically proud of the products we consume: we are more proud to own them. Pre-dating modern technology, artisans created the built environment and the objects we used, and the time and skill taken to create instilled soulfulness and integrity. Maureen Bampton, quoting from *View* magazine, states: 'Craft humanises, it has integrity, it is authentic and has soul – all qualities essential to surviving the twenty-first century.'

Design can have a key role in how consumers engage with fashion products and designers must learn to understand and engage with human unpredictability and complex emotional issues relating to fashion and identity. It could be said that design has been about surface appearance and financial success, and consumers are seen as target markets to exploit. Consumers of fashion may fall in love with an item of clothing, but interest soon fades as an alternative design, a newer version, shape or colour, becomes more desirable.

Chapman suggests this is because design itself does not engage the consumer, that design has no redeeming features to hold attention and fascination; consequently new design and replacement occurs.

So the practice of production and consumption perpetuates. Design is the link between creativity and innovation, and innovation can provide solutions to problems associated with sustainability.

The pleasure fashion can bring can exist with an awareness and responsibility.

164   **Sustainability and
Fashion**

Deconstructing hierarchies
and traditions
Pattern cutting and waste
New horizons

PATTERN CUTTING AND WASTE

6

The pattern cutter can be instrumental in determining how materials are used in the creation of a fashion garment. By creating a pattern that can be reused or that reuses materials itself, the pattern cutter is already restricting the amount of resources required for its production.

HISTORICAL CONTEXT

Garments cut in a traditional way will have very specific pattern shapes, which restrict their reuse unless they are quite large, or are remade from components from other garments into hybrids. For example, in the 1980s it was popular to use the sleeves or body of cable knit jumpers with woven fabric creating hybrid jackets and garments.

In the 1930s, Madeleine Vionnet often cut her garments using simple geometric shapes, mainly squares and rectangles, for the benefit of drape. This could, however, be considered as sustainable practice as the fabric shapes could be reused for other garments. One could argue that 'remodelling' of garments, as in couture, would benefit from having simpler shapes to work with.

USING WASTE MATERIALS

There are many ways to reuse materials and, as mentioned before, the idea of recycling parts or components of garments is not new. Recycling of yarns can usually result in downgrading quality and is referred to as 'downcycling', so using fibres, yarns and garments that maintain or improve quality through reuse is called 'upcycling'.

There are many designers using reclaimed materials from garments and reforming them to create new garments from different sources. In this way, the material is not altered from its original state and can maintain its characteristics and quality.

The shapes and sizes of reclaimed or recycled garment pieces determine what you can do with them, so there are restrictions which can be challenging and that determine what the outcome of the garment will be. The new pattern for these kinds of garments may vary from traditional patterns.

**Right
Mark Liu**
Mark Liu's unique cutting techniques for his 'Zero Waste' collection are designed to save 15% of material on each garment.

Production of multiple garments can often end up with surplus fabric. Cancelled orders and overestimated success reduces production, and waste from this process is called 'post-production waste'. The design company 'From Somewhere' uses end-of-roll post-production waste cloth to create its designs. To create multiple garments from the range of available cloth (that can co-ordinate and be commercially viable) requires joining many fabrics together, and this also means creating the pattern to fit the cloth. The design and pattern allows for mixing different cloth or colours together in varying ratios.

DESIGN, PATTERN CUTTING AND ZERO WASTE

The current system of design, pattern, cut and make is fundamentally wasteful and is being challenged in several ways. A new approach to pattern cutting is 'zero waste', that is, creating patterns that use all the available cloth when cutting the garment. Designer Mark Liu has pioneered this method of cutting, and with his first collection he printed a jigsaw of interlacing lines which created the pattern pieces. These lines were cut and then assembled into garments, using the excess in a decorative way.

CREATING CLOTH TO A SPECIFIC PATTERN SHAPE

A different zero-waste approach is to weave only what is needed, so the pattern pieces are grown onto the loom as fully fashioned bespoke shapes, similar to fully fashioned knit. The weaver Siddhartha Upadhyaya weaves his designs and patterns directly onto the loom. There is no excess, and the fabric pieces are woven according to the size and shape of the pattern pieces.

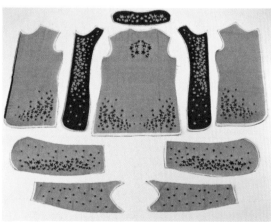

Left
<u>Siddharhta Upadhyaya</u>
In his 'Made to Measure' collection, fashion technologist Siddhartha Upadhyaya devised a method for weaving fabric to the exact shape of the pieces to make up a jacket.

NEW HORIZONS

6

Innovation in sustainable pattern cutting pushes ideas forward and can be seen as a driver for change and exciting new designs. Here, we look at the work of three students, and their quest for sustainable pattern cutting methods.

[Case study]
<u>JANE BOWLER</u>

As we have seen, there are several ways to reuse materials. Many designers use reclaimed materials from older garments, allowing the fabric to be used in its original state and maintaining the fabric's characteristics and quality. Others use pre-cut cloth, allowing the length and width of the reclaimed cloth to determine the pattern of the garment.

But science and technology is offering new opportunities in textile and design development. Using waste from other, less obvious sources, can result in exciting developments, as demonstrated in the work of Jane Bowler:

'My collections highlight my passion to transform inexpensive and mundane materials using unique processes. Hand-dyed plastics and innovative heat-forming techniques make way for a unique approach to fashion design.

In my AW11 collection I made use of discarded and ready-made materials which needed injecting with a new lease of life, finding rolls of unwanted plastics and off-cuts at scrap facilities, which I hand-dyed and heat-treated in order to transform them into exciting garments.

The materials and processes are key to the uniqueness of my designs. Allowing process to define form consequently dictates the aesthetic, texture, pattern and colour of each garment. My collections always begin with my love of materials and the excitement of experimenting with new techniques. This organic process allows the textile to take centre stage and the garment shaping to be influenced by the overriding aesthetics and characteristics of the fabric being created.

In terms of sustainability, my more recent SS12 and AW12 collections continue to explore the transformation of undesirable plastics with the continuing emphasis of designing with longevity in mind, creating beautifully crafted and unique garments that you would want to keep forever, moving away from the ever-growing notion of 'throwaway fashion'.

Above
<u>Blue fringed raincoat</u>
'I love the element of intrigue and disbelief when you mention to someone that a garment is made using shower curtains (blue raincoat AW11), or waste garden furniture fabric (grey tufted raincoat AW11). It's quite magical to think that you can make such things from other people's waste.'

Right
<u>Cutwork PVC jacket</u>
The AW11 collection embraced an innovative heat-forming technique that enabled Jane to cut and emboss the PVC. This process also happened to infuse the plastic with a golden colour, removing the need for dye.

Designers are also exploring how geometry in pattern cutting offers different results and could be explored with a view to sustainable practice. The designer Fong Wong has concentrated on creating designs using a hexagonal pattern shape repeated throughout the garment. A sophisticated computer program enables her to view the garment in 3D before cutting and making it. Her specific manipulation of the hexagons creates textured surfaces and unusual silhouettes, and can create a variety of design possibilities from a set of hexagons.

'Six' is a conceptual collection derived mainly from hexagonal structures. The collection utilizes traditional processes and new technologies in its design and manufacture:

'My research and inspiration comes from nature's hexagonal structures: the honeycomb, and the snowflake. The honeycomb is created from the optimum use of material to surface and space. Snowflakes have infinite possibilities, there are simple structures and complex structures all formed from the basic component of the water molecule. It is from this basis that I derived my process of building the structure that has resulted in the garments illustrated.'

The examples shown here are some of the results of Fong's process, a collection of prototype garments created mainly with hexagons. The process has many possibilities, and has the potential to utilize the 3D design environment where architecture has led the way.

The skirt was the first garment to be created. Starting with a single shape, the design was built by draping the shapes together and then merging sections together to create new forms and structures. Shapes were tessellated; some single and some merged together. Draping processes such as this determine the design rather than allowing a preconceived notion of what the designer wants to create. The final garment was realized in digitally printed silk organza.

Fashion is about change, as new technologies become more readily available, this can only enhance the product development cycle in the future. This collection uses traditional processes and new technologies. The garments use a mix of digitally printed textiles, sublimation printing onto synthetic fabrics, laser cutting and ultrasound techniques.

This method of creating patterns and garments can contribute to sustainable practice, as the hexagonal and other geometric shapes can minimize cloth waste as they interlock together as a jigsaw. The use of CAD and 3D software in the process of the designing can also reduce waste as designs are generated digitally and do not always need paper patterns and toiles to see how the idea works. Applying colour and pattern on cloth using digital printing processes can also minimize dye and print waste as the print is targeted to specific areas and pieces. Ultimately, using renewable, organic or other sustainable textiles completes the sustainable philosophy.

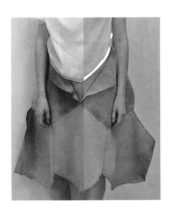

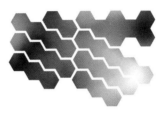

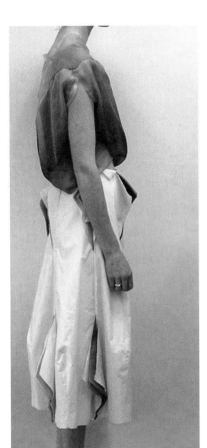
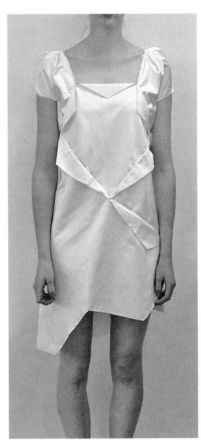

Above
<u>Six Hexagonal Permutations</u>
A process of building in blocks allowed Fong's design to grow organically into something that could not be preconceived.

[Case study]
FEDERICA BRAGHIERI

In trigonometry and geometry, triangulation is the process of determining the location of a point by measuring angles to it from known points at either end of a fixed baseline. The point can then be fixed as the third point of a triangle with one known side and two known angles.

The triangulation technique of pattern cutting was adopted and developed by Stuart Aitken to be used in fashion as an innovative way to create patterns. The body is divided up into a series of triangles which, when assembled, form a 3D garment structure.

Federica Braghieri has experimented with this process and recorded the following:

'The concept of growing geometric structures on the female body to create structured garments, fitted on the body, led me also to different experimentations; starting by drawing geometric shapes directly on the dummy and then creating patterns with the use of the triangulation technique.

My concept was to draw the geometric shapes directly on the dummy, divide them into triangles, and then by measuring a base line and reporting it on paper, measure the two adjacent lines to find the third point with a compass to build my pattern.

The patterns were then scanned and imported in Adobe Illustrator and Gerber Accumark to develop the three-dimensional structures. To create perfectly assembled geometric shapes after laser cutting I explored thermo welding, glue and machining.

The aim of the study was, at first, to generate an innovative process to create structured fashion garments and textures based on geometry, through the use of alternative techniques and technologies.

In order to achieve this aim, I focused on the importance of the body as a main modelling structure, I investigated different opportunities given by 3D and 2D software, and determined the relationship between the use of appropriate materials with innovative technologies of assembly.

The project started with a collaboration with an Italian product designer based in London, Riccardo Bovo, whose latest designs are based on the use of Grasshopper (a graphic algorithm editor). The shape is defined by an algorithm that grows a structure on a guide surface, which is later on created by laser-cutting the pieces and then manually assembled. My idea was to collaborate with him in order to learn this interesting digital technology, usually very popular with architects and interior designers and import it into fashion.

The following question arose: what if I use the human body as my guide surface?

The process I adopted was to import a 3D female model into the software, trim to just the torso, and prepare the mash by reducing the definition to use as a guide surface. Importing this into 'Rhino 3D' enabled me to use Grasshopper applications, where the algorithm generated the geometric structures directly on the body's surface.

The final result was subsequently imported into Pepakura Designer 3 (software developed in Japan to allow the creation of paper craft models from 3D data), in order to unfold the 3D object into the patterns.

Every piece would have not just cut lines, but also engraved lines, to help the material fold into the right position, and would have flaps alternatively positioned, so that it would have a braided look and once laser-cut is then ready to be assembled.

Every piece looks very different from one another and will fit just in a certain position, the assembly is very much like doing a puzzle game, where every piece can be positioned just in one possible place and sustain the other one.'

This is an innovative design process, where everything is designed and developed through software which is not usually used in fashion, where the end result is a piece that will mathematically fit and have the perfect shape and dimensions because it has been developed on the body's surface.

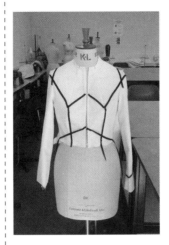

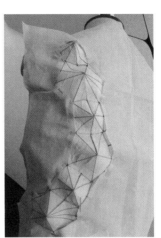

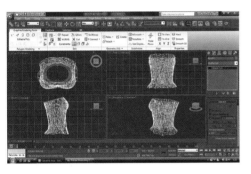

Above
<u>**Innovation through computers**</u>
Federica's idea of using
computers to generate
structures directly on the
human body informed her
entire process for this project.

APPENDIX

CONVERSION TABLE
(metric to imperial)

Every measurement used in this book is listed here, along with its imperial equivalent, to the nearest 64th of an inch.

cm	inches	cm	inches
0.25	$7/64$	10	$3\ 15/16$
0.4	$11/64$	10.8	$4\ 17/64$
0.5	$13/64$	11	$4\ 11/32$
0.75	$19/64$	12	$4\ 47/64$
1	$13/32$	13	$5\ 1/8$
1.27	$33/64$	14	$5\ 33/64$
1.5	$19/32$	15	$5\ 29/32$
2	$51/64$	16	$6\ 5/16$
2.2	$7/8$	17	$6\ 45/64$
2.25	$57/64$	18	$7\ 3/32$
2.5	$63/64$	19	$7\ 31/64$
2.8	$1\ 7/64$	20	$7\ 7/8$
3	$1\ 3/16$	21	$8\ 9/32$
3.3	$1\ 5/16$	21.6	$8\ 33/64$
3.4	$1\ 11/32$	24	$9\ 29/64$
3.5	$1\ 25/64$	26	$10\ 1/4$
4	$1\ 37/64$	27	$10\ 41/64$
4.5	$1\ 25/32$	29	$11\ 27/64$
4.8	$1\ 57/64$	30	$11\ 13/16$
5	$1\ 31/32$	30.5	$12\ 1/64$
5.5	$2\ 11/64$	32	$12\ 39/64$
5.6	$2\ 7/32$	37	$14\ 37/64$
6	$2\ 3/8$	40	$15\ 3/4$
6.5	$2\ 9/16$	43	$16\ 15/16$
7	$2\ 49/64$	46	$18\ 1/8$
7.5	$2\ 61/64$	54	$21\ 17/64$
8	$3\ 5/32$	58	$22\ 27/32$
8.5	$3\ 23/64$	66	$25\ 63/64$
9	$3\ 35/64$	68	$26\ 25/32$
9.5	$3\ 3/4$	84	$33\ 5/64$

GLOSSARY

Allowance
Extra fabric added for the seams of a garment.

Annotations
Written information and instructions on patterns, diagrams and drawings.

Arm scye
The measurement relating to the armhole in a pattern.

Bag-out
Two similar pieces of garment stitched wrong sides together and turned inside out. Used in collars and cuffs, and wherever a double finish is required.

Basic block
A master pattern representing a fundamental shape from which other patterns are derived.

Bias
A diagonal line 45 degrees to the straight and cross-grain, giving optimum stretch and, when combined with gravity, best 'drape'.

Bodice
Front and back upper body of a garment without sleeves.

Boning
A rigid insertion for holding bodice areas up (in controlled fitting such as bustiers and corsets).

Break line
A line where a collar turns and folds back toward the body.

Bust point
The point at which a bust dart ends.

Clip
To reduce the bulk of seam allowances on curves and corners by cutting them away.

Collar
The part of a garment that finishes off a neckline.

Collar fall
Section of a collar that falls away from the neck.

Collar stand
Section of a collar that rises into the neck.

Cross-grain
See bias grain.

Dart
A section of pattern, usually wedge or triangular shape, which takes away excess fabric to shape and fit the body. Side seams can be considered separated side darts.

Double breasted
Extra wide front opening that allows for fastening equally either side of the CF.

Drape
To describe the way fabric falls on a garment or to create controlled fullness and volume in gathers and folds.

Draping (on the stand)
To create a designed garment by manipulating fabric on the tailor's dummy, rather than manipulating a block pattern. Sometimes it can combine both methods.

Drill holes
Marks transferred onto garments from a pattern for sewing and construction guidelines.

Ease
See allowance and tolerance.

Empire line
A bodice which is seamed just below the bust from which the remainder falls.

Eyelet
A small hole in fabric finished with metal rings or stitched to allow drawstrings to pass through.

Facing
A pattern and fabric piece that finishes off raw edges of garments and matches the shape it is finishing, such as necklines, waistlines and areas of garments that cannot be hemmed. It is copied from the original pattern.

Fitting
The way a garment fits on the body, or adjusting the way a garment fits on the body.

Flare
Extra controlled width in a pattern piece.

Flat drawing
See working drawing.

Flexicurve
A bendable linear tool for drawing curves.

Fly
Zipped or buttoned trouser or skirt opening.

Fray
Unravelling of constructed fabrics when cut.

French curve
A pattern cutting tool which helps draw tight and open curves.

Fusing/interfacing
A fabric which stiffens and stabilizes sections of garments. Requires an individual pattern.

Gathers
Extra fabric drawn up tighter with stitching to create fullness.

Godet
A piece of fabric, usually triangular, inserted into a section of a garment, usually the hem, to add flare to that section.

Grading
Increasing or decreasing size using a set of incremental measurements and specific rules or computers.

Grain
The direction of the construction yarns; warp (straight of grain) weft (cross-grain). Most patterns use the straight grain. This prevents the garment distorting and losing shape.

Grainline
The line which indicates the direction of the grain. Patterns are usually placed on the straight grain (warp), parallel to original CF and CB, or in the centre of a pattern piece square to the waist.

Grown-on
Pockets, facings and other parts of a garment that are cut as one with the main pattern but are meant to turn back.

Gusset
A shaped piece inserted into an area to give ease of movement, such as under the arms.

Hem
The end and finish of a garment.

Inset
A piece of fabric or trim placed in a specific place such as a seam.

Interfacing (fusing/ interlining)
A specialist fabric used for strengthening an area of a garment that is either sewn or fused on.

Jetted pocket
A pocket that has bound edges to the opening.

Lapel
Top front edge of a turn back collar.

Lay
The amount of fabric measured in a layplan.

Layering
Cutting away layers of seam at varying widths to minimize bulk.

Layplan
Arranging the pattern pieces to fit fabric width with minimum waste. Used for costing fabric and production. Computers have replaced most hand lay planning.

Lining
A fabric lighter in weight than the main fabric, usually smooth and slippery, and used as an inside casing to the garment. This prevents the garment from sticking to or rubbing up against the body.

Machine stitching
Straight interlock stitching for general seaming and construction of garments. Flat lock stitching for stretch, overlock stitch for finishing edges, buttonholing, hem felling etc.

Mitre
Cutaway corners which will help to avoid bulk.

Mounting
Connecting interlinings to fabric by stitching or fusing.

Muslin
A fine, gauze fabric used for delicate toiles.

Nap (of fabric)
The way in which the fabric fibres fall, affecting how light is reflected from the fabric. Velvet and satin, for example, will have to be cut all the same way.

Needle
Needles are made in various sizes for hand and machine stitching. Machine needles are measured in metric sizes 70–110, with the higher numbers denoting thicker needles. There are various types for different tasks, such as sharps for normal sewing, ballpoint for jersey, leather point and twin needle for double stitching.

Notches
(Balance marks/points) These indicate where seams match. They are important in assembling a garment. Notches are normally spaced and marked differently from piece to piece so that similar shapes do not get mistaken.

Off-grain
Cutting pattern pieces without aligning them to either straight, crosswise or bias grain. Usually this causes the garment to twist and distort if the grain is not uniform or 'true'.

Pattern hook
Twisted hooks available from specialist suppliers used for hanging patterns for storage.

Pattern paper
Pattern paper is available in different weights, plain or spot and cross. If patterns are not computerized then card or plastic is used for production.

Pile
The texture of a fabric which has a raised surface, such as velvet, towelling, fur fabric. The texture has been created by loops or cut loops of yarns.

Piping
An inserted narrow strip of fabric between seams used for decorative purposes, usually contrasting colour or fabric and often with a thin gimp cord inside.

Pivot
Moving a dart without slashing the pattern to a new position.

Placket
An opening finished by fabric, usually by binding on flat or bias grain.

Pleat
A fold of fabric introduced into a pattern for extra width at the hem. Usually if more pleats are introduced they are of equal depth.

Plotter
A machine that is used for digitizing patterns.

Pressing
Heat and steam ironing to finish seams and garments.

Production pattern
A final corrected pattern for industrial purposes. Can be card, plastic or digital.

Quilting
Two fabrics stitched together with a soft layer between to add warmth and decoration.

Rever
Turned-back edge of fabric on a garment, usually in a collar.

Roll line
A line where a collar turns back toward the body.

Rouleau
A narrow, turned-through strip of fabric for straps, button holes and decorative purposes, cut on the bias and which should have a pattern piece.

Ruching
Gathering of material using elasticated thread in the bobbin or drawn up with stitching and held in place. A pattern should indicate the ratio of ruching and have notches to guide it.

Selvedge
The woven edge of a fabric on the lengthwise (warp) grain that finishes the fabric and gives it stability on the loom.

Slash
A cut line in pattern to introduce flare or a gusset, for example. Slash and spread: cutting a line in a pattern and opening out to introduce width.

Sleeve crown (sleeve head)
Upper part of the sleeve that touches the shoulder line.

Squaring lines
See truing-up.

Straight grain
A pattern following the warp (lengthwise yarns) of a fabric.

Suppression
Removing excess in a flat surface such as paper or cloth by forming darts, tucks or seams.

Tacking (basting)
Temporary hand stitches.

Toile
Trial garment to test pattern fit and design. A toile should be made in a similar fabric, including jersey fabric calico (or plain undyed cotton).

Tolerance
Extra allowance added to the body measurements around bust, waist and hip to allow movement.

Tracing wheel
A spiked tool for transferring information on a pattern or toile.

Truing-up (true corners)
Correcting patterns so lines that join (shoulders, armholes, side seams etc.) are square or at right angles to each other. Also smoothing curves and checking lengths of matching seams. Also known as 'squaring'.

Tuck
A small fold introduced into a pattern and garment which is secured by a seam.

Turn-up or turn-back
An added extension to a pattern and garment that folds back upon itself as a cuff.

Vent
An opening as a slit or pleat for movement.

Warp
Yarns that make the base of the cloth and run vertically, these are the most stable yarns in a woven cloth.

Weft
Horizontal yarns that 'fill' the cloth and are at right angles to the warp, these are generally less stable yarns and often give the cloth distinctive character.

Welt
A strip of fabric binding a pocket opening.

Working drawing (technical drawing or flat)
A proportionally scaled line drawing of a garment which indicates all design and construction features clearly. The drawings are flat and without a body and always have a back view and, if necessary, enlarged details.

BIBLIOGRAPHY

Aldrich, W.M. 2008.
Metric Pattern Cutting
(5th Edition)
John Wiley & Sons

Bolton, A. and Koda, H. 2011.
Alexander McQueen:
Savage Beauty
Yale University Press

Chapman, J. 2005.
Emotionally Durable Design:
Objects, Experiences and
Empathy
Routledge

Chunman, D. 2010.
Pattern Cutting
Laurence King

Fletcher, K. 2008.
Sustainable Fashion & Textiles:
Design Journeys
Routledge

Handley, S. 1999.
Nylon: The Manmade Fashion
Revolution
Bloomsbury

Heinberg, R. 2010.
Peak Everything
New Society Publishers

Hodge, B. and Mears, P. 2006.
Skin and Bones: Parallel
Practices in Fashion and
Architecture
Thames and Hudson

Jenkyn-Jones, S. 2011.
Fashion Design
Laurence King

Jones, T. 2008.
Fashion Now 2
Taschen

Koda, H. 2001.
Extreme Beauty: The Body
Transformed
Yale University Press

FURTHER RECOMMENDED
READING

Abling, B. and Maggio K. 2008.
Integrating Draping, Drafting
and Drawing
Fairchild

Aldrich, W. 2007.
Fabric, Form and Pattern Cutting
Blackwell Publishing, 4th, Edition

Armstrong, H.J. 2005.
Patternmaking for
Fashion Design
Pearson Education, 4th Edition

Bray, N. 2003.
Dress Pattern Designing
Blackwell Publishing

Burke, S. 2006.
Fashion Computing: Design
Techniques and CAD
Burk Publishing

Dormonex, J. 1991.
Madeleine Vionnet
Thames & Hudson

Fischer, A. 2009.
Basics Fashion Design:
Construction
AVA Publishing

Nakamichi, T. 2010.
Pattern Magic
Laurence King

Sato, H. 2012.
Drape Drape
Laurence King

Szkutnicka, B. 2010.
Technical Drawing for Fashion
Laurence King

Tyrrell, A. 2010.
Classic Fashion Patterns
Batsford

Ward, J. and Shoben, M. 1987.
Pattern Cutting and Making Up:
The Professional Approach
Butterworth-Heineman

SUSTAINABLE FABRIC
SUPPLIERS

Akin Tekstil
www.akintekstil.com.tr
Organic cotton and recycled
fibres.

Apac Inti Corpora
www.apacinti.com
Recycled denim.

Ardalanish Weavers
www.ardalanishfarm.co.uk
Native-breed wool and naturally
dyed.

Asahi Kasei Fibres Corp
www.asahi-kasei.co.jp
Recycled PET, retrieved polyester
fibres for suede alternatives.

Avani Kumaon
www.avani-kumaon
Hand spun and woven silk,
natural dyes, solar powered
closed loop production.

Bhaskar Industries
www.bhaskarindustries.com
Innovative blends of cotton denim
for large-scale production.

Bossa Denim
www.bossa.com
Denim production with eco
principles.

Burce Tekstil
www.burce.tr
Performance fabrics using
organic cotton and certified
fabrics, prints and dyes.

Cornish Organic Wool
www.cornishorganicwool.co.uk
100% organic wool yarn.

Dashing Tweeds
www.dashingtweeds.co.uk
Hi-tech tweeds using GOTS
certified dyes and processes.

Delcatron
www.delcatron.be
European linen with controlled chemicals with no heavy metals.

Ecotintes
www.ecotintes.com
Natural and eco-dying.

ES Ltd
www.es-salmonleather.com
Eco-produced leather from salmon skin (a by-product of the fishing industry).

Eurolaces
www.eurolaces.com
100% organic macramé lace, eco-production.

Guangzhou Tianhai Lace Co.
www.gztianhai.com
Laces using recycled polyester and nylon, organic cotton, modal and cupro, eco-production.

Gulipek
www.gulipek.com
Natural cellulose-based fabrics such as tencel, cupro, silk, linen meeting EU regulations.

Hemp Fortex Industries
www.hempfortex.com
Eco-production of hemp and other fabrics.

Herbal Fab
www.herbalfab.com
Handspun and woven vegetable dyed fabrics, eco-production and community support.

Holland & Sherry
www.hollandandsherry.com
Merino, fine and worsted wools, waste water treatment.

Jasco
www.jascofabrics.com
Environmentally sensitive fabrics, organic cotton, low-impact dyes.

Jiangsu Danmao
www.verityfineworsteds.co.uk
Wool and recycled fibres, animal welfare and developing biodegradable polyester.

Jiangxing Jiecco
Helen@jiecco.com
Raw organic fibres for a range of woven and knitted fabrics.

Klasikine Tekstile
klasikinetekstile.lt
Eco-produced European linen.

Libeco-Lagae
www.libeco.com
European linen, low-impact dyes.

Lurdes Sampaio SA
www.ismalhas.com
Innovative organic fibre combinations, e.g. crabyon, ramie, modal, tencel c and kapok, recycled cotton and bypass re-dying.

Mahmood Group
www.mahmoodgroup.com
Eco-organic cotton.

Northern Linen
www.northern-linen.com
Organic linen.

Organic Textile Company
www.organicccotton.biz
Suppliers of organic and fair-trade cotton and bamboo fabrics.

Pastels SAS
www.pastels.fr
Organic, recycled and ethically produced fabrics.

Peru Naturtex
www.perunaturtex.com
Fair-trade Peruvian organic cotton and Alpaca knit and woven fabrics, natural dyes.

Pickering International
www.picknatural.com
Importers and wholesalers of organic and natural fibre textiles in USA.

Singtext/Scafe
www.singtex.com
Recycled coffee grounds combined with a range of fibres and recycled polyester for performance and insulation fabrics.

Sophie Hallette
www.sophiehallette.com
Lace and gossamer tulle using traditional and modern methods following Oeko-Tex guidelines.

Svarna
www.svarna.com
Luxurious gold muga silk, hand woven khandi cottons and other traditional textiles with low impact carbon footprint.

Swiss Organics
www.swissorganicfabrics.ch
Organization representing Swiss organic cotton producers.

Tessitura Corti
www.tessituracorti.com Recycled polyester performance textiles.

The Natural Fibre Company
www.thenaturalfibre.co.uk
Organic, naturally dyed wool, eco production.

TYMAXX INC
www.tymaxx.com.tw
Recycled polyester fabrics, low impact dyes, eco production

Weisbrod
www.weisbrod.ch
Organic silks, eco and social principles, fully traceable supply chain.

Winfultex
www.winfultex.com.tw
Recycled polyester, modal and organic cotton for sports and casual fabrics.

Page numbers in italics refer to illustrations

3D body scanners 17

A-line shape 64
above-waist fitting, trousers
    148–151
aesthetics 163
Aldrich, Winifred 12
Alexander McQueen *111*
anthropometry 16
asymmetrical curved darts
    40–41
awls 28

Balenciaga *141*
balloon shape 102–107
Bampton, Maureen 163
basic blocks 32
batwing sleeves 72, 106
bishop sleeves 58
blocks 12, 18
basic 32
    bodice 20, 33
    skirt 22, 32
    sleeve 21, 33
    trouser 22
bodice blocks 20, 33
bodice panel lines 44–47
body
    measuring 18–22
    shape 16–17
    size 16–17
Bounsall, Jacquie 15
Bowler, Jane 166, *167*
Braghieri, Federica 170, *171*
bust darts 34

CAD/CAM (Computer Aided
    Design and Computer Aided
    Manufacture) 12
CF and inset panel darts 39
Chapman, Jonathan 162, 163
Chapurin *63*
circles 136
cocoon shape 98–101
collars 128–135

Compaing, Guillaume 17
computers 12, 16
consumers 8
consumption 162
cuffs 126–127
curves (tools) 28, 29
cutting mats 29

darts 32, 34–43
    asymmetrical curved
        40–41
    bust 34
    CF and inset panel 39
    dartless design 42–43
    diamond inset 38
    flare 54
    waist 36
deconstructing garments 12
designers 8
designs
    interpreting 14
    seasonal 12
diamond inset darts 38
digitized patterns 12
dolman sleeves 72, 124–125
dome shape 88–93
Donna Karan *63*
draping 12

Emilio de la Morena *63*
Eton collars 131

Farrow, Mia *17*
fashion design 8
Faulkener, Ruth 14
Fawcett, Farah *17*
female ideal shape 16
fitted sleeves 113
fitting 32
flare, adding 52–55
fly front zip openings 159

gathering 36–37, 104
Giannini, Frida 102
glossary 173–175
Goh, Tse *63*
Grable, Betty 16
grown-on sleeves 72, 118–125

half and half, blocks 33
Harcus, Zoe 76–77, *76*
Heinberg, Richard 163
hems 49, 58–59
Herchovita, Alexandre *62*
Herrera, Caroline 82
high-stand collars 135
hourglass shape 82–87

interpreting designs 14
inverted triangle shape 68–71

jeans 150

kaftans 72
Khalique, Kashaf 86–87, *86*
kimono sleeves 120–122
Kinder Aguggini *129*
Klein, Anne 17

lantern shape 94–97
linear shape 64–67
linings 105
Liu, Mark *164*, 165
Louis Vuitton *63*

Manish Arora *63*
Mazzola, Margherita *13*
McQueen, Alexander 14, 140
measuring 16, 18–22
Monroe, Marilyn *17*
Moss, Kate *17*
Mukhtar, Nadine 137, *137*

natural waistline 20
Nicole Farhi *63*
Nielsen, Brigitte 17

offset panel lines 46–47
one-piece collars 130–133
Ozaki, Yuichi *3*

Packard, Vance 163
panel lines (panels) 44–49
pattern cutter's role 14
pattern drills 28
pattern hole punches 29
pattern hooks 29

pattern masters 28
pattern notchers 28
patterns 12
peg-top skirts 56–57
Peter Pan collars 130
Petrini, Carlo 162
pins 28
pleats 144–147
pockets 156–158
post-production waste 165
Prada 63
Pugh, Gareth 63

raglan sleeves 118–119
raising sleeve crown 115
Rodriguez, Narcisco 26
ruffles 136
rulers 28, 29

scalpels 29
scissors 28
seasonal designs 12
semi-fitted sleeves 112
set-in sleeves 112–117
set squares 29
shape 62–107
    balloon 102–107
    cocoon 98–101
    dome 88–93
    female ideal 16
    hourglass 82–87
    inverted triangle 68–71
    lantern 94–97
    linear 64–67
    square 72–77
    trapeze 78–81
shirts 114, 134
short puffed sleeves 59
'signature' style 12
size charts 24
sizing 17
skirts
    balloon 104
    blocks 22, 32
    panels 48–49
    peg-top 56–57
    underskirts 105
slash and spread 52

sleeves 110–127
    batwing 72, 106
    bishop 58
    blocks 21, 33
    cuffs 126–127
    grown-on 72, 118–125
    set-in 112–117
    short puffed 59
Smit, Anna 92–93, 92
square shape 72–77
squared shoulders 115,
    116–117
Saint Laurent, Yves 140
stationery 29
style lines 50–51
sustainability 161–165

tailor's chalk 28
tailor's dummies 12
tape 28
tape measures 28
tools 26–29
tracing wheels 28
trapeze shape 78–81
troubleshooting
    darts 42
    flare 55
    shape 75, 85, 91
    sleeves 113
    style lines 51
    trousers 154
trousers 140–159
    above-waist fitting 148–151
    below-waist fitting 152–153
    blocks 22
    finishing 156–158
    pleats 144–147
    standard fit 142
    tighter fit 150–151
two-piece collars 134–135

underskirts 105
unpickers 29
Upadhyaya, Siddhartha 165,
    165

Vionnet, Madeleine 164
volume, adding 56–59

waist darts 36
waistlines 20, 36, 104
waste 162, 164–165
waste materials 164
Westwood, Vivienne 110, 140
Wong, Fong 168, 169

yokes 54

zero waste 165
zips, trousers 159

ACKNOWLEDGEMENTS

This book started out as a solo project, but soon became a collaboration of students and designers, illustrators, photographers, students, industry suppliers and well wishers. It is for aspiring designers and pattern cutters such as Genevieve Spencer who have a passion for the subject.

Thanks to:
My editor Leafy Cummins must get a special mention for her endless support and patience.

A special thank you to Michael Crawley for taking on the Adobe® Illustrator® work, despite having no knowledge of patterns. I'm sure he's now aware of neck points and grain lines!

My son Alex Parish for finding a photographer Milo, model Jess and illustrator Michael.

To the student and designer contributors for sharing their inspiring work.

Maggie Doyle for her fabulous illustrations.

Jess grant for the loan of her body for the photos.

Milo Belgrove for arranging the studio and photoshoot.

Jacquie Bounsall for the interview.

Specialist suppliers 'Kennet and Lindsell' for the loan of the mini model.

Phil Wheeler from ethical suppliers 'organiccotton.biz' for the organic cotton and bamboo silk.

The 'sustainableangle.org' for producing a booklet of sustainable fabric suppliers.

My family and friends, especially Rob, who put up with me during this time.

This book is dedicated to my mother.

The publisher would like to thank Debbie Allsop, Clare Culliney Rebbecah Pailes-Friedman, Janet Robinson and Juliana Sissons, for their reviews of the manuscript.

IMAGE CREDITS

Body measurements and toile photography by Milo Belgrove Diagrams and technical drawings by Pat Parish and Michael Crawley

Cover: Federica Braghieri (London College of Fashion) designer, image photographed by Oscar Roca

P3: Yuichi Ozaki, photograph by Andy Espin

P9: Jane Bowler (Royal College of Art), Photography by Joanne Warren, Model Grace Du Prez

P13: Margherita Mazzola (UCA Epsom), courtesy of UCA Epsom

P16/17, 1890s-1910s: Wikicommons
P16/17, 1920s: Wikicommons
P16/17, 1930s: Wikicommons
P16/17, 1940s: 20TH CENTURY FOX / THE KOBAL COLLECTION
P16/17, 1950s: Wikicommons
P16/17, 1960s: COLUMBIA / THE KOBAL COLLECTION
P16/17, 1970s: Wikicommons
P16/17, 1980s: MGM/UA / THE KOBAL COLLECTION / SCHAPIRO, STEVE
P16/17, 1990s and beyond: Wikicommons

P63, 111, 129, 141: © Chris Moore, Catwalking.com

P64, 65, 68, 69, 72, 73, 78, 79, 82, 83, 88, 89, 94, 95, 98, 99, 102, 103: Maggie Doyle

P76/77: Zoe Harcus

P86/87: Kashaf Khalique (Cavendish College)

P92/93 Anna Smit (Royal College of Art), photographs by Christina Smith

P137: Nadine Mukhtar (Winchester School of Art), BA (Hons) Fashion Design

P164/165: Science & Society Picture Library

P167: Jane Bowler (Royal College of Art), Photography by Joanne Warren, Model Grace Du Prez

P169: Images by Fong Shan Wong

P171: Federica Braghieri (London College of Fashion) designer, images photographed by Oscar Roca

Publisher's note

The subject of ethics is not new, yet its consideration within the applied visual arts is perhaps not as prevalent as it might be. Our aim here is to help a new generation of students, educators and practitioners find a methodology for structuring their thoughts and reflections in this vital area.

AVA Publishing hopes that these **Working with ethics** pages provide a platform for consideration and a flexible method for incorporating ethical concerns in the work of educators, students and professionals. Our approach consists of four parts:

The **introduction** is intended to be an accessible snapshot of the ethical landscape, both in terms of historical development and current dominant themes.

A selection of **further reading** for you to consider areas of particular interest in more detail.

The **framework** positions ethical consideration into four areas and poses questions about the practical implications that might occur. Marking your response to each of these questions on the scale shown will allow your reactions to be further explored by comparison.

The **case study** sets out a real project and then poses some ethical questions for further consideration. This is a focus point for a debate rather than a critical analysis so there are no predetermined right or wrong answers.

**Required Reading Range
Working with ethics**

**Lynne Elvins
Naomi Goulder**

Ethical: awareness/ reflection/ debate

Introduction

Ethics is a complex subject that interlaces the idea of responsibilities to society with a wide range of considerations relevant to the character and happiness of the individual. It concerns virtues of compassion, loyalty and strength, but also of confidence, imagination, humour and optimism. As introduced in ancient Greek philosophy, the fundamental ethical question is: what should I do? How we might pursue a 'good' life not only raises moral concerns about the effects of our actions on others, but also personal concerns about our own integrity.

In modern times the most important and controversial questions in ethics have been the moral ones. With growing populations and improvements in mobility and communications, it is not surprising that considerations about how to structure our lives together on the planet should come to the forefront. For visual artists and communicators, it should be no surprise that these considerations will enter into the creative process.

Some ethical considerations are already enshrined in government laws and regulations or in professional codes of conduct. For example, plagiarism and breaches of confidentiality can be punishable offences. Legislation in various nations makes it unlawful to exclude people with disabilities from accessing information or spaces. The trade of ivory as a material has been banned in many countries. In these cases, a clear line has been drawn under what is unacceptable.

But most ethical matters remain open to debate, among experts and lay-people alike, and in the end we have to make our own choices on the basis of our own guiding principles or values. Is it more ethical to work for a charity than for a commercial company? Is it unethical to create something that others find ugly or offensive?

Specific questions such as these may lead to other questions that are more abstract. For example, is it only effects on humans (and what they care about) that are important, or might effects on the natural world require attention too?

Is promoting ethical consequences justified even when it requires ethical sacrifices along the way? Must there be a single unifying theory of ethics (such as the Utilitarian thesis that the right course of action is always the one that leads to the greatest happiness of the greatest number), or might there always be many different ethical values that pull a person in various directions?

As we enter into ethical debate and engage with these dilemmas on a personal and professional level, we may change our views or change our view of others. The real test though is whether, as we reflect on these matters, we change the way we act as well as the way we think. Socrates, the 'father' of philosophy, proposed that people will naturally do 'good' if they know what is right. But this point might only lead us to yet another question: how do we know what is right?

Further reading

AIGA
Design Business and Ethics
2007, AIGA

Eaton, Marcia Muelder
Aesthetics and the Good Life
1989, Associated University Press

Ellison, David
Ethics and Aesthetics in European Modernist Literature: From the Sublime to the Uncanny
2001, Cambridge University Press

Fenner, David E W (Ed)
Ethics and the Arts: An Anthology
1995, Garland Reference Library of Social Science

Gini, Al and Marcoux, Alexei M
Case Studies in Business Ethics
2005, Prentice Hall

McDonough, William and Braungart, Michael
Cradle to Cradle: Remaking the Way We Make Things
2002, North Point Press

Papanek, Victor
Design for the Real World: Making to Measure
1972, Thames & Hudson

United Nations Global Compact
The Ten Principles
www.unglobalcompact.org/AboutTheGC/TheTenPrinciples/index.html

A framework for ethics

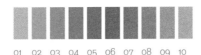

01 02 03 04 05 06 07 08 09 10

Your specifications
What are the impacts of your materials?

In relatively recent times, we are learning that many natural materials are in short supply. At the same time, we are increasingly aware that some man-made materials can have harmful, long-term effects on people or the planet. How much do you know about the materials that you use? Do you know where they come from, how far they travel and under what conditions they are obtained? When your creation is no longer needed, will it be easy and safe to recycle? Will it disappear without a trace? Are these considerations your responsibility or are they out of your hands?

Using the scale, mark how ethical your material choices are.

01 02 03 04 05 06 07 08 09 10

You
What are your ethical beliefs?

Central to everything you do will be your attitude to people and issues around you. For some people, their ethics are an active part of the decisions they make every day as a consumer, a voter or a working professional. Others may think about ethics very little and yet this does not automatically make them unethical. Personal beliefs, lifestyle, politics, nationality, religion, gender, class or education can all influence your ethical viewpoint.

Using the scale, where would you place yourself? What do you take into account to make your decision? Compare results with your friends or colleagues.

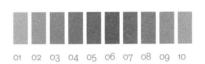

01 02 03 04 05 06 07 08 09 10

Your creation
What is the purpose of your work?

Between you, your colleagues and an agreed brief, what will your creation achieve? What purpose will it have in society and will it make a positive contribution? Should your work result in more than commercial success or industry awards? Might your creation help save lives, educate, protect or inspire? Form and function are two established aspects of judging a creation, but there is little consensus on the obligations of visual artists and communicators toward society, or the role they might have in solving social or environmental problems. If you want recognition for being the creator, how responsible are you for what you create and where might that responsibility end?

Using the scale, mark how ethical the purpose of your work is.

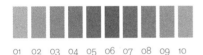

01 02 03 04 05 06 07 08 09 10

Your client
What are your terms?

Working relationships are central to whether ethics can be embedded into a project, and your conduct on a day-to-day basis is a demonstration of your professional ethics. The decision with the biggest impact is whom you choose to work with in the first place. Cigarette companies or arms traders are often-cited examples when talking about where a line might be drawn, but rarely are real situations so extreme. At what point might you turn down a project on ethical grounds and how much does the reality of having to earn a living affect your ability to choose?

Using the scale, where would you place a project? How does this compare to your personal ethical level?

Case study

One aspect of fashion design that raises an ethical dilemma is the way that clothes production has changed in terms of the speed of delivery of products and the now international chain of suppliers. 'Fast fashion' gives shoppers the latest styles sometimes just weeks after they first appeared on the catwalk, at prices that mean they can wear an outfit once or twice and then replace it. Due to lower labour costs in poorer countries, the vast majority of Western clothes are made in Asia, Africa, South America or Eastern Europe in potentially hostile and sometimes inhumane working conditions. It can be common for one piece of clothing to be made up of components from five or more countries, often thousands of miles apart, before they end up in the high-street store. How much responsibility should a fashion designer have in this situation if manufacture is controlled by retailers and demand is driven by consumers? Even if designers wish to minimise the social impact of fashion, what might they most usefully do?

Is it more ethical to create clothing for the masses rather than for a few high-ranking individuals?

Is it unethical to kill animals to make garments?

Would you design and make a feather cape?

Fashion is a form of ugliness so intolerable that we have to alter it every six months.

Oscar Wilde

Feather capes

Traditional Hawaiian feather capes (called *'Ahu'ula*) were made from thousands of tiny bird feathers and were an essential part of aristocratic regalia. Initially they were red ('Ahu'ula literally means 'red garment') but yellow feathers, being especially rare, became more highly prized and were introduced to the patterning.

The significance of the patterns, as well as their exact age or place of manufacture is largely unknown, despite great interest in their provenance in more recent times. Hawaii was visited in 1778 by English explorer Captain James Cook and feather capes were amongst the objects taken back to Britain.

The basic patterns are thought to reflect gods or ancestral spirits, family connections and an individual's rank or position in society. The base layer for these garments is a fibre net, with the surface made up of bundles of feathers tied to the net in overlapping rows. Red feathers came from the *'i'iwi* or the *'apapane*. Yellow feathers came from a black bird with yellow tufts under each wing called 'oo'oo, or a mamo with yellow feathers above and below the tail.

Thousands of feathers were used to make a single cape for a high chief (the feather cape of King Kamehameha the Great is said to have been made from the feathers of around 80,000 birds). Only the highest-ranking chiefs had the resources to acquire enough feathers for a full-length cape, whereas most chiefs wore shorter ones which came to the elbow.

The demand for these feathers was so great that they acquired commercial value and provided a full-time job for professional feather-hunters. These fowlers studied the birds and caught them with nets or with bird lime smeared on branches. As both the *'i'iwi* and *'apapane* were covered with red feathers, the birds were killed and skinned. Other birds were captured at the beginning of the moulting season, when the yellow display feathers were loose and easily removed without damaging the birds.

The royal family of Hawaii eventually abandoned the feather cape as the regalia of rank in favour of military and naval uniforms decorated with braid and gold. The *'oo'oo* and the *mamo* became extinct through the destruction of their forest feeding grounds and imported bird diseases. Silver and gold replaced red and yellow feathers as traded currency and the manufacture of feather capes became a largely forgotten art.